HEIGHTS AND FLIGHTS

Martha K. Resnick

Carolyn J. Hyatt

Sylvia E. Freiman

STECK-VAUGHN
ELEMENTARY · SECONDARY · ADULT · LIBRARY

A Harcourt Company

www.steck-vaughn.com

About the Authors

MARTHA K. RESNICK is an experienced elementary teacher, formerly a Reading Resource Teacher with the Baltimore City Schools. She has served as a cooperative practice teacher, training student teachers from many colleges. Mrs. Resnick received her master's degree in education at Loyola College.

CAROLYN J. HYATT has taught elementary, secondary, and adult education classes. She was formerly a Senior Teacher with the Baltimore City Schools. Mrs. Hyatt received her master's degree in education at Loyola College.

SYLVIA E. FREIMAN has taught primary and upper elementary grades. She has conducted teacher in-service classes, supervised student teachers, and participated in curriculum planning. Mrs. Freiman received her master's degree in education at Johns Hopkins University.

Reading Comprehension Series

Wags & Tags

Claws & Paws

Gills & Bills

Manes & Reins

Bones & Stones

Swells & Shells

Heights & Flights

Trails & Dales

Acknowledgments

Illustrated by Rosemarie Fox-Hicks, Ray Burns, and David Cunningham

Cover design Linda Adkins Design

Cover photograph © Comstock

All Photographs used with permission. Page 90 © 1988 Kenji Kerins

ISBN 0-8114-1351-9

Contents

1 From the time of the cave people and down through the ages, humans could only get from place to place by walking. These trips were long and difficult. People saw the birds flying quickly from place to place. How they envied those birds!

Then people found a way to travel faster. They rode on animals. They also had the beasts pull their vehicles. Still, the high-flying birds got to places faster. The humans were jealous.

This jealousy made people experiment with learning to fly. Why should people be stuck on the ground? They were more intelligent than birds. People made wings and jumped from high places, but they never flew. They just sank like rocks.

In ancient times, the Greeks made up a myth about a boy named Icarus who constructed wings of feathers held together by wax. Icarus dared to fly with his wings and went so high that he got too close to the sun. The heat melted the wax, and poor Icarus plunged back to earth.

This myth was the Greeks' way of warning humans that their gods would punish them if they tried to soar through the air. Flying was only for insects, birds, and Greek gods.

In the 1700s, people began to believe that, with the aid of science, they could do anything. In France, the Montgolfier brothers, Etienne and Joseph, tried once more to imitate the birds.

One day, as Joseph sat by his fireplace looking at the fire, he suddenly realized that the ashes floated up the chimney. Aha! He had it! Hot smoke made the ashes light enough to fly.

To experiment, Joseph filled a bag with smoke and put it in the fireplace. The bag floated up the chimney. The Montgolfier brothers did this experiment over and over. It always worked.

In June 1783, the Montgolfiers made a big balloon of linen and paper. They filled it with smoke from a fire. They let it go. Up, up it went! It reached a height of 6,000 feet and landed a mile and a half away. It was a miracle! Instantly, the two brothers became famous.

At the same time, other French scientists were experimenting with **hydrogen,** a gas lighter than air. In August 1783, a hydrogen-filled balloon went up 3,000 feet and floated fifteen miles.

The Montgolfiers continued to experiment and soon understood that it was hot air, not smoke, that made their balloons soar. Then the King of France, Louis XVI, commanded them to send up a hot-air balloon in front of his palace. A huge crowd came to watch.

To make the event more spectacular, the brothers had the idea of decorating the balloon and attaching a basket to it. In the basket were a duck, a rooster, and a sheep, the first air passengers. The balloon took off and rose with no trouble.

The flight lasted eight minutes, but the balloon did not float very far. It came down near the palace. The waiting spectators were thrilled to see the passengers were fine. A joker reported that the beasts were in good physical shape, but they weren't speaking to each other.

Aha! Humans were envious again. The animals had flown! They wanted to fly, too!

On January 7, 1785, John Jeffries, an American, and Jean-Pierre Blanchard, a Frenchman, set out to fly across the English Channel from England to France.

Jeffries and Blanchard did not realize that in winter it was so cold that the air in the balloon would not stay hot. When they reached the middle of the English Channel, the air in the balloon cooled and contracted. The balloon began to sink down toward the waves.

"We must make the balloon lighter, so it can rise!" exclaimed Blanchard.

Jeffries and Blanchard started throwing things from the balloon's basket. First, they got rid of their food. Then, they took the decorations off the balloon. Still, the basket was sinking toward icy water. Next, off went the heavy ropes that were used to tie down the balloon when it was on the ground. Then they tossed out the anchors. Soon there was nothing left to get rid of but their clothes.

Out went their shoes, then coats, jackets, hats, shirts, and stockings! Just in time, the balloon drifted into a patch of warmer air. Back up it soared and carried them to the coast of France.

People cheered. An American and a Frenchman had successfully crossed the English Channel in a hot-air balloon. The heroes were greeted with shouts and cheers. They were shivering but happy heroes as they climbed out of the balloon wearing only their underwear.

King Louis did not care how they were dressed. He rewarded them with medals and some money.

 A Underline the correct answer for each question.

1. What special event led to people's ability to make a balloon fly?
   a. Icarus's flight with wings made from eagle feathers and wax
   b. King Louis XVI's contest to see who could invent the best balloon
   c. Montgolfier's discovery that hot smoke made ashes rise
   d. Jeffries and Blanchard tossing their food and clothes out of their balloon

2. Why were ropes always carried in balloons?
   a. as part of the decorations
   b. to tie the pilot and the passengers into the basket
   c. as something to burn to keep the air or the hydrogen hot
   d. to tie down the balloons on the ground

3. Which would be the best title for this article?
   a. Birds Teach Humans to Fly   b. King Louis XVI Flies
   c. A Basket of Animals   d. Humans Learn to Fly

4. Why was hydrogen used to make balloons fly?
   a. Air is lighter than hydrogen.   b. Hydrogen is lighter than air.
   c. Hydrogen is heavier than air.   d. Hydrogen is easy to find.

5. Why did the Montgolfiers put a basket under their balloon?
   a. to put more hydrogen in the balloon
   b. to carry tools to repair the balloon
   c. because King Louis XVI ordered them to do it
   d. to carry some animals

6. Why do you think the Montgolfiers put animals in the balloon's basket?
   a. to see if the basket was strong enough
   b. to see if the animals liked flying
   c. to see if the animals got along
   d. to see how safe flying was

7. What is the story of Icarus called?
   a. a myth   b. a mystery
   c. a fairy tale   d. a humorous story

8. Why did humans envy birds?
   a. Birds had beautiful feathers.
   b. Birds could travel farther and faster.
   c. Birds could find homes more easily.
   d. Birds could get away from their enemies more easily.

9. How did the King reward Blanchard and Jeffries?
   a. by giving them land
   b. by giving them a new balloon
   c. by letting them live in the palace
   d. by giving them medals and money

10. What is hydrogen?
    a. water   b. a solid   c. a gas   d. a metal

B Write the correct word on the line to complete each sentence.

spectacular   constructed
soar   plunged
vehicle   jealous
imitate   decorations
command   myth
      contracts

1. To order is to _____.

2. To envy is to be _____.

3. A truck is a heavy _____.

4. The palace was _____ of fine marble.

5. A colorful flying balloon is a _____ sight.

6. They watched the eagle _____ to the top of the cliff.

7. The diver _____ into the sea.

8. The story of Icarus is a Greek _____.

9. To act like someone else is to _____ that person.

10. When the air in a balloon gets cold, it _____.

C The events below tell how human beings tried to imitate birds in order to learn how to fly. The sentences are not in the correct order. Look back in the story and then number the sentences in the right sequence. The first step is numbered for you.

_____ a. Joseph Montgolfier saw hot air pushing ashes up a chimney.

_____ b. Two men crossed the English Channel in a hot-air balloon.

_____ c. The Montgolfiers attached a basket to the hot-air balloon and sent animals up in it.

__1__ d. Humans saw the swift, easy flight of birds and envied them.

_____ e. People made wings and jumped from high places but could not fly.

_____ f. The Montgolfiers filled a big balloon with smoke, and it soared into the air.

D Read the story. In what order did the things happen? Write the letter of the correct answer next to each question.

At first, hot-air ballooning was not as popular in the United States as in France. Then, Benjamin Franklin sent reports back to the United States of the wonderful balloons in France. In 1793, Jean-Pierre Blanchard came to the United States and flew in a balloon from Philadelphia to New Jersey. Nine years before that, a brave 13-year-old boy, Edward Warren, had made the first recorded hot-air balloon flight in the United States. An American balloon which had a steam engine and wings was built in 1869. It flew, but had no passengers.

_____ 1. What came first?

_____ 2. What came second?

_____ 3. What came third?

_____ 4. What came fourth?

a. A balloon with wings and a steam engine was built.

b. Franklin reported on balloons in France.

c. Balloons were useful when France was at war.

d. A thirteen-year-old boy was the first American to travel in a hot-air balloon.

e. Blanchard came to the United States.

E Read the story. Then draw a line under the correct answer to each question.

One of the bad things about balloons was that they could only go in the direction that the wind was blowing. Soon many people were trying to find ways to steer balloons. First, Blanchard tried using oars and paddles to guide his balloon. He was not successful. Next, a man tried to train eagles or pigeons to pull a balloon through the air. The birds were unwilling. In 1852, a man named Giffard attached a steam engine to his hydrogen-filled balloon. It could be steered by the pilot, but was very dangerous because hydrogen caught fire easily. Next, people invented electric engines so pilots could steer balloons, but the batteries were too heavy to carry in the balloons. Finally, gasoline motors were put into balloons. They were not as flammable as hydrogen engines, were much lighter than batteries, and gasoline was readily available.

1. When did someone try to teach eagles to pull balloons?
   a. after electric engines were invented
   b. before steam engines were tried
   c. after batteries were too heavy for the balloons

2. When did Giffard attach a steam engine to a balloon?
   a. after Blanchard used paddles
   b. before Blanchard tried oars
   c. after 1860

3. When were gasoline engines used to steer balloons?
   a. before steam engines
   b. before electric engines
   c. after electric engines

4. What steered the hot-air balloon before the Montgolfier brothers sent people up in the air?
   a. hydrogen motors
   b. steam engines
   c. nothing

F Events in stories are often caused by something that happened before. This is called **cause** and **effect**.

>   **cause:** It is raining.
>   **effect:** The ground has become wet.

It is easier to work out the order in which things happen if you remember that the cause comes first and the effect follows. When putting story or article events in order, keep that clue in mind. Often, many effects are produced by one cause. Circle the letters of all the effects that could be produced by each cause given. Cross out all the effects that could not be produced by the cause.

1. Because people have always looked for ways to make work easier,

   _____

   a. they learned to use fire to cook and to heat their homes.
   b. they disliked trying new inventions.
   c. they began to use plows.
   d. they trained animals to help them work.
   e. they worked less and slept more.

2. Because the early balloons could not be steered, _____
    a. passengers did not know where they would land.
    b. passengers did not know how long they would be flying.
    c. pilots had to use two-way radios.
    d. pilots had to use maps to guide the balloon.
    e. the passengers had to be brave to go up.
    f. people used the stars to direct the balloons.

3. Because they could see the sun low in the evening sky, _____
    a. they knew it would soon be night.
    b. they knew they were traveling towards the east.
    c. they knew they were traveling towards the west.
    d. they knew it would be dark.
    e. they knew the sun would soon set.
    f. they knew it would soon be dawn.
    g. they knew the moon and the stars would soon be seen in the east.

G Choose the correct cause for each effect. Write the letter in the sentence.

Causes
a. Because sound travels slower than light,
b. Because small streams move together and join,
c. Because the sun can affect human skin,
d. Because dinosaurs lived on earth millions of years before humans,
e. Because the stars are very far away,
f. Because jet airplanes were invented,

---

1. _____, they must be studied with a telescope.

2. _____, rivers are formed.

3. _____, people can travel long distances in less time.

4. _____, no person has ever seen one.

5. _____, lightning is seen before thunder is heard.

2

As their airplane was preparing to land, Charley exclaimed, "This is going to be the most exciting thing in our lives! For the rest of our days, we will be bragging about seeing two games of the 1989 World Series."

Mom laughed, "Charley will probably bore his grandchildren to death by telling them this story over and over."

The Brent family came from a small town in West Virginia. They were all serious baseball fans. They read newspaper sports stories, listened to the games on the radio, and sat glued to the T.V. set.

Charley's sister, Ellen, was still amazed at Dad's good luck. He had won tickets for the third and fourth games of the World Series. Mr. and Mrs. Brent could not believe their good fortune. Somehow, they found the time and the money and, on October 16, 1989, were on their way to California.

San Francisco delighted the whole family. They did all the things tourists did. They rode the cable cars up and down the steep hills, ate crab meat at Fisherman's Wharf, and drove across the Golden Gate Bridge.

By 5:00 P.M. on Tuesday, October 17, the Brents were in their box seats in Candlestick Park waiting for game Number 3 to start. The Oakland A's had beaten the San Francisco Giants in the first two games. Ellen and her father, who always cheered for the underdog, were hoping that the Giants would win, but Charley and his mom were sticking with the A's. About 60,000 other spectators were around them, all waiting for the Gatlin Brothers to sing the Star Spangled Banner and for the game to start.

9

At exactly 5:04 P.M., the excitement rose to new heights. But it was not sports excitement. Something strange was occurring at Candlestick. The windows in the enclosed box where the Brents sat began to shake violently. The high orange light towers, that were to illuminate the playing field when darkness fell, began to vibrate and sway back and forth. Pieces of stone fell from the top deck across the way. The Brents felt the ground shift and tremble beneath their feet.

"What's happening?" shrieked many voices.

Some spectators had brought radios, and they turned them on. News announcers were repeating the words, "Earthquake! Earthquake!"

Even with all the trembling and swaying, there was little damage to Candlestick Park. The earthquake did not seem too serious. Soon the trembling stopped. The players stood on the field, some of them joined by their families from the stands.

Mr. Brent held on to his family. As the tremors lessened, most people seemed to be calm. Forty minutes later, they were informed the game was canceled. The throng was told their tickets would be honored whenever and wherever the World Series was continued.

It was not until the Brents were on the way back to their hotel in their rented car that they understood the horror that earthquakes can bring. A large bridge had collapsed and smashed vehicles were everywhere. Police officers and firefighters directed Mrs. Brent, who was driving, how to get back to their hotel.

What a scene greeted the Brents when they got back. The building had not been damaged, but there was broken glass all over. There was no gas, electricity, or water. People with walkie-talkies and flashlights were going from room to room in the hotel to help the guests.

It was amazing how people were getting the courage to take care of each other. The hotel manager served cold food and bottled water to the guests.

Some helpers found stores open where they could get candles, batteries, flashlights, and canned foods and brought them to those who needed help.

"This has been a nightmare," said Ellen.

Mom said, "We're very lucky! We're all well and we are all together."

Dad laughed for the first time in hours. "We will certainly be boring our friends, our grandchildren, and our great-grandchildren with our tales of how we survived the '89 San Francisco earthquake!"

 A Underline the correct answer for each question.

1. Where did the Brents live?
   a. in a town somewhere in California
   b. in a small town in West Virginia
   c. in another country
   d. in the state of Hawaii

2. Where were the Brents during the earthquake?
   a. in their hotel   b. at Fisherman's Wharf
   c. on the airplane   d. in a stadium

3. Why were the Gatlin Brothers there?
   a. to be umpires in the game   b. to sell hotdogs and popcorn
   c. to collect the tickets   d. to sing to start the game

4. What is the best title for this story?
   a. What Tourists Do in San Francisco
   b. Why World Series Games Are No Longer Held
   c. An Interruption to the World Series
   d. Living Without Gas, Electricity, and Water

5. What made the Brents decide to come to California?
   a. They wanted to visit the children's grandparents.
   b. They were going to a movie.
   c. They wanted to buy a new house.
   d. They won some tickets.

6. Where did Dad get the tickets?

    a. in a bingo game   b. in a cereal box

    c. at a ball game   d. The story did not explain.

7. Why couldn't some of the guests leave their hotel rooms after the earthquake?

    a. Elevators cannot run without electricity.

    b. The hotel had collapsed.

    c. The hotel was badly damaged.

    d. The locks on the door were jammed.

8. When did the Brents find out about the damage the earthquake caused?

    a. when their plane landed

    b. when they rode the cable car

    c. when they drove from the game to their hotel

    d. when they got to their seats at Candlestick Park

9. What does it mean that the tickets would be honored when the games were continued?

    a. The people who survived would get medals.

    b. The spectators would be given free food.

    c. Tickets could be used in the future.

    d. The spectators would be given season tickets for the baseball games.

10. How did the Brents get back to their hotel from the stadium?

    a. on the subway   b. by automobile

    c. on cable cars   d. by railroad

11. Why did the Giants decide to have a game on the day of an earthquake?

    a. It was more exciting to play in an earthquake.

    b. They didn't. No one knows when earthquakes will happen.

    c. The weather people said the earthquake was coming a week later.

    d. The only thing that stops the World Series is rain.

12. What does underdogs mean?

    a. the stomachs of dogs   b. the favorites in the day's game

    c. players under the stands   d. those who are not expected to win

13. Why were the Giants the underdogs that day?

    a. They arrived late for the game.

    b. They had won the first two games.

    c. They had lost the first two games.

    d. Many of their best players had been injured.

B Hit some home-runs. Score by matching the correct words to each definition. Write them next to the meanings.

stadium	violent	tourists	illuminated	spectators
tremor	vibrate	throng	courage	shrieked
canceled	survived	heights	occurring	World Series

1. visitors who travel to see a place _____

2. to shake _____

3. lived through _____

4. lit up _____

5. happening, or taking place _____

6. a place where sports events take place _____

7. people watching sports events _____

8. screamed or shouted _____

9. very strong or powerful _____

10. a shaking movement that follows
    an earthquake _____

11. called off _____

12. games to see which major league team
    is better _____

13. high places _____

14. a large group crowded together _____

C Often in a paragraph, one sentence states the **main idea.** This sentence is called a **topic sentence.** It can be found anywhere in the paragraph. Read the paragraphs below. Then underline the topic sentence in each paragraph.

1.   Engineers have learned from earlier earthquakes. They have discovered ways to make safer structures. Because of this new information, loss of life and property has been reduced.

2.   Safe bridges, roads, and buildings are often placed on solid rock, the best kind of land for structures. Engineers now know it is important not to place different parts of a structure on two different kinds of subsoil. For example, they do not place one section on weaker landfill and the other part on strong rock. Soil brought down by rivers and deposited near their mouths is the worst to build on. Structures are no longer built on loose gravel and certain kinds of clay that turn liquid when shaken. The most important factor in controlling earthquake damage has been the erecting of new structures on the proper land.

3.   Today, engineers stress strength and flexibility when building large structures. The materials used, such as reinforced concrete and steel frames, prevent much damage during earthquakes. Steel rods placed in the concrete blocks make them stronger and safer. The newer ways of building and bracing houses, bridges, dams, and roads have been proved to resist earthquake damage.

4.   Today, all parts of a large building must be connected so they support one another. In that way, the entire structure will vibrate evenly, preventing one part from falling and causing damage to others. In earthquakes, no one section will feel more stress than the others. Buildings can sway in strong winds and earth tremors but remain undamaged. Earthquake resistant buildings, in which all sections are connected, cost more, but they save money in the long run. So modern skyscrapers all over the world are built in this way.

D The **details** in a paragraph support the main idea. Read the paragraphs below and look at the pictures. Underline the main idea in each paragraph. On the lines after each paragraph, write the detail sentence that describes the picture.

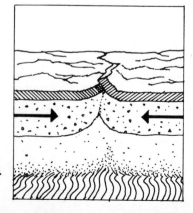

1.   Pieces of the earth's crust, called **plates,** are far under the ground. They move and grind against each other. They slip over and under one another. If they meet and bump, they cause tremors in the earth. Large plates grinding violently or separating suddenly cause earthquakes.

_____

_____

14

2.   Just as in earthquakes, volcanic eruptions occur when the earth's plates bump into each other and separate. Sometimes when the plates separate, the melted, fiery rock in the center of the earth bubbles up through the crack with great force. Then all the melted rock, flame, gas, ashes, and stones erupt into the air. The melted rock, called **lava,** comes pouring out. This is a volcanic eruption.

_____

_____

_____

3.   The Japanese word for a harbor wave is **tsunami** (tsoo nah me). **Tsunami** is now part of all languages. Earthquakes occurring anywhere set off huge waves under the ocean. These waves, called **tsunamis,** are over 100 feet high and travel 500 miles an hour. When they strike land, they destroy everything in their paths. Sometimes **tsunamis** hit near the place of the earthquake, but often they occur hundreds of miles away from the earthquake's center. Many more people are killed by the giant waves than by the earthquake tremors.

_____

_____

_____

4.   To protect yourself during an earthquake, first try to switch off all lights to prevent electrical fires in the walls. Find a solid, strong piece of furniture such as a desk or a table and crawl under it, so falling glass or plaster will not hit you. Or you can stand in the doorway between two rooms. Doorways are braced to take stress. When the earthquake is over, go outside to a wide open space in case there are aftershocks. Stay away from downed wires.

_____

_____

_____

Read the paragraphs below carefully. Do all the sentences give more information about the topic? If a sentence does not support the main idea of the paragraph, it is **extraneous.** Draw a line through every extraneous sentence.

1.   Some people think that watching the behavior of animals can help predict an earthquake. It is said that the beasts know before humans that the earth will soon be vibrating. Some spectators claim that dogs barking without stopping signals an earthquake. Tigers, lions, leopards, pandas, and deer in China became very excited before a volcano erupted. Rats have been seen to leave their hiding places in large groups before the tremors disturbed humans. Before a forest fire, a huge army of ants carrying their eggs marched away from the woods.

2.   On the Richter Scale, numbers show how strong the tremors of earthquakes are. People do not feel the tremors unless they register 2 or above on the scale. Hurricanes are identified by the female and male names assigned to them. Some dishes are unbreakable even in earthquakes. At 5 on the Richter Scale, buildings shake. Heavy furniture turns over, chimneys fall, and walls may collapse at 6.2 on the Richter Scale. At 7, underground pipes may break. A reading of 8 on the Richter Scale can mean an area is completely destroyed. The surface of the earth is usually calm and comfortable.

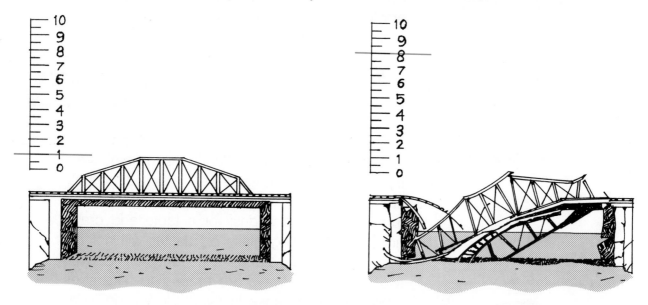

3.   Do not run out into the street during an earthquake. Pieces of falling stones, bricks, and concrete may hit you as you leave the building. Hurricanes often cause more damage than earthquakes. If your home has a tile roof, stay inside because tiles are the first to fall in tremors, and their weight makes them dangerous weapons. Outdoors, do not stand close to buildings, trees, or telephone poles. When a volcano erupts, lava pours down its sides.

3

After several days of summer storms and strong downpours, it was a relief to Brian, Ilene, and Debbie to walk on the beach again. They awoke at dawn and ran outside to watch the sun paint the sky aqua, peach, and pink as it rose in the east.

How good it felt to run on the damp sand next to the ocean. Their footprints crossed and recrossed as they jumped and jogged about. Only a few adults riding horses and walking dogs appeared this early on the beach.

Ilene, as usual, walked toward the row of bushes growing at the far end of the beach away from the water. She had seen rabbits there last week. Suddenly, her feet sank into the watery sand. She tried to lift them, but couldn't. They seemed to be stuck as if in deep mud.

"Debbie! Brian!" shouted Ilene to her sister and brother.

The more she pulled, the further she seemed to sink. Her legs were in the sand up to her knees. Such a thing had never happened to Ilene before.

Debbie and Brian, hearing Ilene's yells, raced towards her.

"It looks as if you're in quicksand," said Brian. "I wish I could remember more about it."

"Quicksand?" echoed Ilene. "We studied that in science class, but I don't know how to get out of it. I'm afraid! It may keep pulling me down."

The children were motionless with fear, trying to decide what to do.

17

"Go get help! Get Mom and Dad!" Brian told Debbie.

"No!" said Ilene. "Don't leave me! Stay with me! I'll need both of you to pull me out."

A small group of adults from the beach had gathered. No one knew what to do. One man tried to wade to Ilene. His feet got stuck, too. He was close enough for several people to grab him and yank him out.

Two people ran to call the police and the emergency crew. The rest watched Ilene, unable to do anything but stare.

"She's not sinking any further," called out one woman. "That's a good sign!"

Then, a strange figure appeared. It was a young boy of about eleven years who rode his horse on the beach every morning. No one ever talked to him because he kept at a distance, but all recognized him. He always dressed in a cowboy hat and boots. Ilene's family called him the Cowboy.

"What's going on?" he questioned as he cautiously approached the growing circle around Ilene.

When informed of Ilene's danger, he stared at the quicksand for a minute. Then he smiled, as if there was nothing to fear.

"Don't try anything, Kid," yelled a man. "Wait for the emergency crew!"

Still atop his gray and white horse, the cowboy said nothing. He grabbed the rope from his saddle, made a lasso, and swung around.

"Everybody get ready to help pull!" he ordered.

The lasso flew out into the sand twice, missing Ilene. The cowboy moved his horse to another part of the sand so he faced Ilene's back. Again he twirled the lasso, tossed it, and finally it settled around Ilene's shoulders.

"Put it around your waist!" the cowboy directed, remembering that her weight would be easier to pull.

With shaking fingers, Ilene obeyed. Then the cowboy tightened the lasso and started to pull. Everyone grabbed a part of the rope and helped tug.

The first couple of tries, Ilene didn't move.

"You have to relax, Ilene," said Debbie. "Make yourself as limp as possible. Don't worry; we have you."

The force of the pulling knocked Ilene onto her back. Everyone froze in fear.

"It's okay," said the cowboy. "She's better off on her back because it evens out her weight on the surface. Now, everyone, grab on again and PULL!"

This time, Ilene was pulled onto solid ground. Brian and Debbie hugged her. The crowd cheered.

Two police cars and an ambulance arrived a couple of minutes later. The rescuers were praising each other. Everyone thought the cowboy and his horse were heroes.

The cowboy smiled, lifted his hat, and said he had to be going. Ilene said to her brother and sister, "It looks as if we'll be getting up at dawn tomorrow to find our new friend to thank him."

 Underline the correct answer for each question.

1. What is the story mainly about?
    a. how quicksand is formed
    b. a careless girl
    c. the rescue of someone in danger
    d. the police cars and an ambulance

2. Which of these happened first in the story?
    a. The cowboy twirled his lasso.
    b. A man tried to rescue Ilene.
    c. The eleven year old boy lifted his hat.
    d. Ilene walked towards the bushes.

3. Which of these happened last in the story?
    a. Ilene fell over backward.
    b. The man's feet left the quicksand.
    c. The children ran on the beach.
    d. Ilene stepped into the quicksand.

4. How do you think the cowboy knew so much about quicksand?
    a. He worked with the emergency crew.   b. His father was a doctor.
    c. His mother was a policewoman.   d. The story does not say.

5. Why do you think Ilene was rescued so quickly?
    a. The police came.   b. She froze in fear.
    c. Everyone worked together.   d. She weighed very little.

6. When did this story take place?
    a. at sunset   b. at sunrise
    c. midday   d. shortly after midnight

Brian said, "When we go back to school in the fall, I'm certain the teacher will ask us to write about something interesting we did this summer. How can we do it without really understanding what quicksand is?"

Debbie said, "Let's go to the library and learn more about quicksand."

B Use dictionary skills to answer the following questions.

1. Circle the guide words for the page that might contain *quicksand*.

    a. | quote   quotient | b. | quiver   quiz |

    c. | quench   quiet | d. | quack   queen |

2. Read this section of a dictionary page and answer the following questions.

> **quaint**   **quill**
>
> **quaint** (kwānt) *adj:* unusual or odd
> **quan·ti·ty** (kwăn'-tĭ-tē) *n:* a number or an amount
> **quar·rel** (kwŏr'-ĕl) **1** *n:* an angry fight **2** *v:* to find fault
> **quar·ry** (kwŏr'-ē) *n* **1:** something that is hunted; prey **2:** place from which to get stone
> **queen** (kwēn) *n* **1:** a female ruler; the wife of a king **2:** a playing card with the picture of a queen
> **ques·tion** (kwĕs'-chŭn) **1** *n:* something that is asked **2** *v:* to ask
> **quick** (kwĭk) *adj:* fast
> **quick·sand** (kwik'-sănd) *n:* a loose, deep, wet sand deposit in which a heavy object or person may sink
> **quill** (kwĭl) *n* **1:** a feather **2:** a kind of writing pen

20

1. How many meanings are given for the word *quarrel*? _____

2. Which words are both a noun and a verb? _____

3. What meaning did the dictionary give for *quicksand*? _____

   _____

4. A feather is also called a _____ .

5. Which meaning of the word *quarry* is used in this sentence?

   > The marble was bought from a **quarry** in New England.

   _____

6. How many syllables does the word *quantity* have? _____

7. What noun would be used in place of *a fox that is chased by hunters*?

   _____

8. Which of these words could be used as synonyms for *quick*?

fast	quiet	rapid
speedy	quack	swift

   _____

9. Which word would be used for *a person who runs a country*?

   _____

   The children had learned in school where to locate information. They went to the library to get a textbook called *The Soil Under Your Feet.*

   Since the whole book was about soil, they had to use the index to find their topic. This is what they knew about the index.

   1. The *index* is at the end of a book.
   2. The index is arranged in alphabetical order.
   3. It is used as a quick way to see if a special topic is to be found in the book.
   4. The index can also tell all the information about a special topic that can be found in the book.
   5. It can tell on which pages the information is located.

C This is part of the index of a book. Read it and answer the questions.

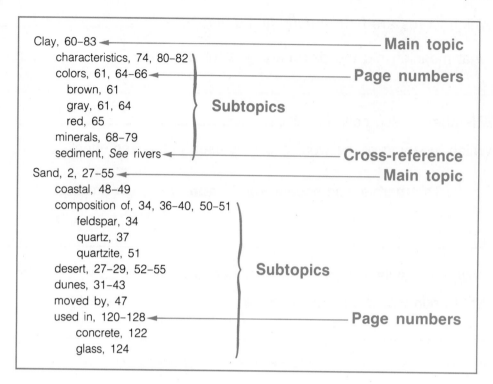

1. Which pages have information about desert sands?

   _____

2. On which pages can information be found on the minerals found in clay?

   _____

3. On which pages can information be found on sand dunes?

   _____

4. How many subtopics are found under *Sand*?

   _____

5. This book also tells about the topic *Loam*.
   Underline the place where it would be found.
   a. before *Clay*
   b. between *Clay* and *Sand*
   c. after *Sand*

6. Why does it say **See rivers** next to *sediment*?

   _____

D For further information the children turned to the encyclopedia. Look at the volumes and answer the questions.

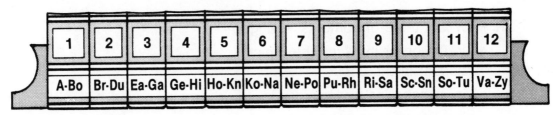

1	2	3	4	5	6	7	8	9	10	11	12
A-Bo	Br-Du	Ea-Ga	Ge-Hi	Ho-Kn	Ko-Na	Ne-Po	Pu-Rh	Ri-Sa	Sc-Sn	So-Tu	Va-Zy

1. How many volumes are in this set of encyclopedias? _____

2. In which volumes might they look for information on *desert sands*?

   _____   _____

3. In which volume might they find information about *quicksand*? _____

4. What beginning letters are on the three volumes in which you might find information on *palomino* and *appaloosa* horses?

   _____   _____   _____

From their searching for information the children learned these facts about *quicksand*:

1. Any sand can become quicksand. It does so when the water rises from under the sand and spreads the sand grains far apart.
2. The fine, deep, watery sand is no longer firm. It cannot support heavy weights. It is a liquid.
3. Quicksand looks the same as the nearby ordinary solid sand.
4. When caught in quicksand, a person should not struggle. The only thing to do is to try to lie flat on one's back. A body spread out over a wider surface of sand will not sink. The person floats on the quicksand.

E Read the following sentences. Write **T** if the sentence is true, **F** if it is false, and **N** if not enough information is given.

_____ 1. Quicksand is dry soil that pulls small objects down.

_____ 2. Quicksand is fine, deep, liquid sand.

_____ 3. When a person is lying flat, his/her body can float on the quicksand.

_____ 4. Another name for *quicksand* is *livesand*.

_____ 5. The bones of dinosaurs are found in quicksand.

_____ 6. Pulling and pushing one's feet in the quicksand helps people get out.

_____ 7. When caught in quicksand, the best thing to do is to lie flat.

_____ 8. Quicksand is solid.

Underline the correct answer for each question. If you need to see a table of contents, look at the one in this book.

1. How is a table of contents arranged?
   a. in the order in which the topics appear in the book
   b. in alphabetical order
   c. Neither answer is correct.

2. How is an index arranged?
   a. chapter by chapter
   b. in alphabetical order
   c. Neither answer is correct.

3. Which one would be arranged like this?

   Chapter I —Origin of the Horse. 3
   Chapter II —Kinds of Horses .28
   Chapter III—Diseases of Horses. 47

   a. the table of contents
   b. the index
   c. neither of them

4. Which one is a list of words, their meanings, and their pronunciations?
   a. the table of contents
   b. the index
   c. neither of them

5. Which one divides the words into syllables?
   a. index
   b. dictionary
   c. table of contents

6. Which one is arranged in alphabetical order?
   a. table of contents
   b. encyclopedia
   c. neither of them

4

The clop of horses' hooves and the shouts of people rang through the forest. Hidden in a woodcutter's hut, the twins, Enid and Edward, giggled. They were delighted to think that they had caused all this excitement!

Some soldiers dismounted for a closer inspection of the ground.

"I think it went up the hill," said one man.

"Sire!" called out a soldier. "Hoofprints! The unicorn came in this direction."

Lord and Lady Bracey and their soldiers prepared to follow the tracks. How eager they were to find that never-before-captured beast, the unicorn!

In their hiding place, the twins could barely control their laughter. They knew that the hoofprints hadn't been made by the magic feet of the imaginary animal.

Lord John ordered, "Let's go around the hill to head it off before it reaches the fields."

Suddenly Lady Isabel Bracey cried, "Wait! We're wasting our time. These cannot be the hoofprints of a unicorn."

"What do you mean, my Lady?" asked the steward, the man who took care of the castle.

"See! The beast is wearing iron horseshoes," explained Lady Isabel. "These iron shoes are just like those made by our blacksmith!"

"Fooled again!" exclaimed Lord John Bracey. "'Tis the work of the smith's wicked children once more!"

The steward suggested, "This time they should be punished."

Suddenly, the twins quit laughing. At last, one of their tricks was discovered before they fled far from the scene. It took only a few seconds for the soldiers to find Enid and Edward in the hut. A pale gray horse with a wooden horn tied to its head nibbled the grass nearby.

"And that unicorn is really **my** own gray mare, Canter!" shrieked Lady Isabel. "Oh, you, wicked, WICKED, WICKED children! You made all the soldiers leave the castle without protection to chase a fake unicorn."

In the year 1280 the lord who owned the land ruled over all who lived there. Enid, Edward, and their parents were dragged into the Great Hall of Lord Bracey's castle for punishment.

"If you were not the best blacksmith in the country," thundered the steward to the twins' father, "I would have all of you thrown off this property."

"How old are you, children?" questioned Lord John.

Enid and Edward bowed. "Nine years old, Sire!" they said together.

"Why aren't they working from sunrise to sunset like everyone else?" asked Lady Isabel.

"Forgive them, my Lady," begged the smith. "They are quick, good workers. Edward is so fast in the forge that we often finish all the horseshoes ahead of time. He will some-day be the best smith in all of Britain."

"What about the young girl?" asked the steward.

"Enid is just the same, Sire," explained their mother. "She spins thread faster than any woman in the village. Then she plays pranks when her work is finished."

The steward interrupted, "It is true, Sire. They are among the best workers in your service. But I also have a list of their wrongdoings."

Enid and Edward trembled. How had the sneaky steward discovered all their pranks. He even knew that they were the ones who spread the story of the fire-eating dragon in the lake. He knew how they had faked the smoke supposedly floating from the dragon's nostrils.

"Not a seed was planted near the lake for two weeks," read the steward. "The villagers were too frightened of the dragon. They even left the sheep unguarded, and wolves killed one."

Enid realized now was the time to speak up. "Please, Sire," she said to Lord John. "We only made the horse look like a unicorn because the one you have on your shield and the one on the castle banner are so beautiful."

Edward followed his sister's lead. "We only wanted to make you and Lady Isabel happy. We wanted you to think you had a real unicorn to match your flag."

"You have been so good to us," continued Enid, "that we wanted to do something for you!"

Lord and Lady Bracey's anger melted.

The smith looked at his children. "Now no one will ever believe you two. If you need help, people will think it is another of your tricks!" he whispered.

For punishment, the steward commanded the twins to work outside the castle walls gathering firewood whenever they finished their regular work. Thus it happened that one night they returned late to the castle. The drawbridge was raised. There was no way to cross the moat, a ditch filled with water that circles the castle.

27

In those days poor children were used to sleeping outdoors at times. Enid and Edward stretched out in the darkness hoping that soon someone important would need to
enter or leave the castle. Then the guards would lower the
drawbridge.

The twins were almost asleep when they heard a strange
sound. Peering through the darkness, they saw a small boat
in the moat near the back square towers of the castle. The
guards high in the towers did not see or hear what was
happening. Silently, the twins watched for what seemed like
hours. Men in the boat appeared to be working with
something at the base of the right tower.

When Edward and Enid told their father the next morning
about what they had seen, he laughed. When they told the
captain of the guards, he growled, "Ha! Ha! Another one of
your jokes." When they informed the steward, he sneered
and said, "You cannot fool me this time!"

For the next ten nights, the twins stayed outside the
castle to watch the strangers. It seemed as if the men in the
boat were loosening a stone on the corner of the tower just
above the water.

Like all poor people in 1280, the twins and their parents
depended on Lord and Lady Bracey's soldiers to protect
them. They, in turn, helped the castle owner fight off enemies

when there was danger. If the castle were captured, all the inhabitants would be killed, so everyone had to work together. Edward and his sister guessed that the men in the boat were enemy soldiers. No one, however, would listen to the children.

The next day Edward and Enid checked the inside of the tower to see what the strangers had done. They crept into the dark cellar and felt their way through a passage into the bottom of the tower. What a shock it was to discover that thirty large stones were loose and ready to be pushed out!

"They can bring in a whole army late at night in boats," explained Edward fearfully. "They will creep in through this hole and take our soldiers by surprise."

The twins tried to warn Lady Isabel of the danger.

She replied, "I cannot believe a word you say."

"Someone inside the castle may be helping the enemy," said Enid to Edward. "Let's watch from inside. If we find out who it is, someone may believe us."

That night they tiptoed through the cellars armed with two pieces of iron from the forge. This time, they could hear the sound of the enemies' tools picking at the stones. A dark shadow stood inside the tower speaking to the strangers.

"Tomorrow night the opening will be large enough for the attack," they heard a familiar voice stating. "Have all the boatloads of soldiers here by two hours past midnight. We will surprise Lord Bracey while he sleeps. Then I will be the ruler of the castle and the land!"

The twins were amazed. It was the steward, Lord John's knight and keeper of the castle. He was helping the enemy. In her surprise, Enid cried out.

The steward whirled around. Sword in hand, he rushed at the children. They stepped back and raised their iron bars to protect themselves. It was an uneven fight. The blacksmith's children were quick and small. The steward was large, and the narrow passage was too crowded. He could not raise his sword. Enid and Edward knocked him down.

Their noise and shouting brought the guards down into the cellars. The guards told Lord Bracey that the castle was being attacked. The adults no longer thought the twins were playing another trick on them.

Realizing that they had saved the lives of everyone in the castle made the twins happy. They had also learned the importance of having other people trust them.

 A Underline the correct answer to each question.

1. At what time were the enemies going to enter the castle?
   a. at dawn
   b. at midnight
   c. at 2 A.M.
   d. at 2 P.M.

2. Which of these would be the best title for the story?
   a. Trust Must Be Earned
   b. How Castles Are Built
   c. Life in England
   d. Fast Work

3. For what were Lord and Lady Bracey hunting?
   a. a rare animal
   b. their lost unicorn
   c. animals to kill for food
   d. an imaginary animal

4. Why didn't the adults trust the twins?
   a. They were lazy and careless.
   b. They helped Lord John's enemies.
   c. They stole from and cheated people.
   d. They had played too many tricks.

5. From what you have read, which of these sentences is not true?

    a. The people crossed the moat on a drawbridge.

    b. A moat was a deep ditch filled with water.

    c. The unicorn crossed the drawbridge to enter the castle.

    d. A moat surrounded the castle.

6. What happened last?

    a. The twins pretended to have seen a dragon.

    b. The steward rushed forward with his sword.

    c. Lady Isabel went on a hunt for a unicorn.

    d. No one believed the twins.

7. How did Lady Isabel discover that the hoofprints were not those of a unicorn?

    a. Unicorns do not have hooves.

    b. Because they looked like a regular horse's hoofprints.

    c. Unicorns have smaller hooves than horses.

    d. Unicorn hoofprints are square in shape.

8. How had the twins made the adults think there was a unicorn nearby?

    a. by taking pictures of the animals

    b. by fastening a wooden horn onto a horse

    c. by putting a costume on a cow

    d. by dressing in a unicorn costume

9. How did the enemy plan to capture the castle?

    a. by breaking down the drawbridge

    b. by bringing troops by boat to climb the outside of the tower

    c. by digging a tunnel under the castle and entering the Great Hall

    d. by entering through a hole made in the bottom of a tower

10. Which of these events happened after the unicorn prank?

    a. The twins put a horn on a mare.

    b. Lord John and Lady Isabel hunted for a unicorn.

    c. The twins had to gather firewood after finishing work.

    d. The twins saw smoke coming from the dragon's nostrils.

11. What job did the twins' father have?

    a. He was the steward of the castle.

    b. He was a blacksmith.

    c. He was the captain of the guard.

    d. He was a farmer.

B Read each sentence below. Choose the correct word form from the word box to complete each sentence.

───────── Word Box ─────────

suggest	suggests	suggested	suggesting
	suggestion		

1. Lord John would not accept the steward's _____ to keep the drawbridge down all day long.

2. A year before, Lady Isabel had _____ that more guards be stationed on the walls.

3. As Mother was _____ that Enid should spin more carefully, she was interrupted.

4. Edward was able to _____ some faster ways to heat the iron.

5. Lord John only _____ you go hunting. You must decide.

6. Lady Isabel _____ that Edward entertain his friends in the Great Hall.

C Climb the tower. Match each word with its synonym. Write the synonym beside the word.

1. commanded _____

2. female horse _____

3. inspect _____

4. fled _____

5. moat _____

6. dismounted _____

7. captured _____

8. banner _____

9. scene _____

10. well-known _____

a. look at
b. familiar
c. got off
d. location
e. ordered
f. ran away
g. caught
h. property
i. hint
j. mare
k. ditch
l. flag

D Read the story below. Use the words in dark type to label the parts of the drawing.

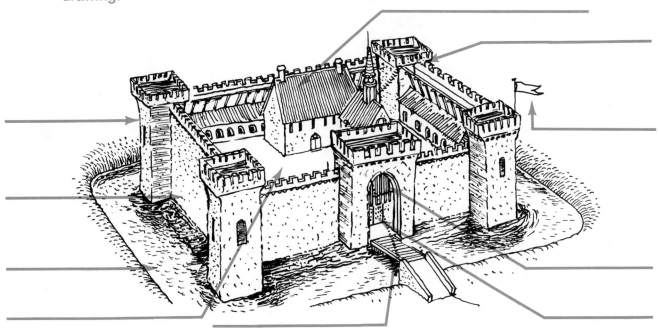

Lord and Lady Bracey were invited to the king's castle. With their steward and soldiers, this is how they entered the well-protected building.

As the party approached the castle, they first saw the four square **towers**. Between the towers stretched a thick, strong stone **wall**. Along the wall and the tops of the towers were **battlements**. The king's soldiers could fire arrows at enemies and then hide behind the battlements for safety.

From the highest tower flew the special **banner** of the king. The guards in the towers checked to see if the Braceys were friends. Then they lowered the **drawbridge** so the Braceys could cross the deep **moat**.

At the end of the drawbridge, the Braceys faced a heavy iron gate. It was called the **portcullis**. Guards raised it by turning a large wheel. Behind the gate was a heavy wooden **door**. Guards raised a huge bar to open it.

The Braceys then entered a **courtyard**. Again guards inspected them by looking through tiny arrow slits in the walls. Finally, Lord and Lady Bracey were led inside the castle to the **Great Hall**.

E Write the correct word for each picture or sentence below. Then write the letter of the correct meaning of the word.

tower:
    a. a high building
    b. to rise above

forge:
    c. a furnace where iron is heated to be shaped
    d. to shape metal as a blacksmith does
    e. to make a fake object
    f. to move forward

light:
    g. not heavy
    h. a means of seeing in the darkness
    i. to land on something
    j. to make it possible to see in the darkness
    k. pale

1. Bees _____ on the flowers. _____

2. The man had to _____ more horseshoes. _____

3. Start the fire in the _____. _____

4. Use this torch to _____ the way through the tunnel. _____

5. The large package is _____ enough to carry easily. _____

6. She wore a _____ gray coat. _____

7. See how the oak trees _____ over the bushes. _____

8. The soldiers began to _____ ahead. _____

F Suffixes are endings added to root words to change the meaning. Adding the suffix **ion** to some verbs changes them into nouns. Circle the correct word to complete each sentence. Look carefully at each root word.

Examples:

Lady Isabel made an *inspection* of the hoofprints. Edward made a *suggestion* about how to capture the enemies.

1. The pipe _____ was loose.

    connection   convention   collection

2. His _____ made us laugh at him.

    locations   inspections   actions

3. A light will help you discover the _____ of the loose stones.

   election   connection   location

4. They invited everyone by sending _____.

   actions   invitations   conditions

5. After Lord John's _____ of the tower, I was ordered to clean it.

   inspection   instruction   invitation

6. The new _____ was stopped after high winds knocked down the walls.

   location   construction   information

7. The soldiers marched in the _____ of the river.

   election   direction   inspection

8. To learn how to shoot with a bow and arrow, you must follow my _____.

   directions   elections   constructions

G Study the map below. Then answer the following questions. Write the letter next to the question.

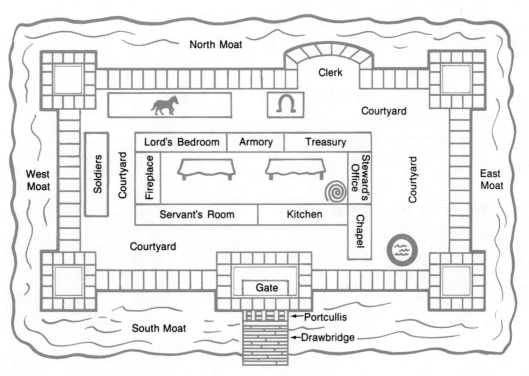

1. Where is the forge? _____
   a. next to the stables
   b. next to the treasury
   c. in the moat

2. Where are the quarters for the soldiers? _____
   a. next to the well
   b. near the east wall
   c. near the west wall

3. Where is the armor kept? _____
   a. next to the fireplace
   b. the north end of the Great Hall
   c. in Lord Bracey's bedroom

4. How many towers are there? _____
   a. four   b. two   c. three

5. Where is the well? _____
   a. by the spiral stairs
   b. the south end of the courtyard
   c. next to the stables

6. Why is the smith located by the stables? _____
   a. to be near the drawbridge
   b. to be near the horses
   c. to be near the east wall

7. Where do the people go to pray? _____
   a. to the treasury
   b. to the chapel
   c. to the Lord's bedroom

8. Where do the servants sleep? _____
   a. next to the moat
   b. close to the kitchen
   c. close to the forge

SKILLS REVIEW (Stories 1-4)

A Choose the correct words to complete the following sentences.

direct	directly	directed	directing	direction

1. A balloon can only move in the _____ the wind takes it.

2. A bag of smoke rose _____ up the chimney.

3. When they felt the tremor, he _____ them to a safe place.

4. The village was _____ in the way of the lava.

5. When the bridge collapsed, firefighters had to _____ vehicles to other streets.

6. People had to find ways to steer a hot-air balloon in a certain _____.

occur	occurs	occurred	occurring	occurrence

7. Scientists still cannot predict when an earthquake will _____.

8. The _____ of an earthquake stopped the World Series.

9. Tsunami waves _____ after earthquakes.

10. An earthquake is a terrible _____.

11. It _____ to the cowboy that he could lasso Ilene.

12. Edward told his father what had _____.

13. The twins knew what was _____ in the castle.

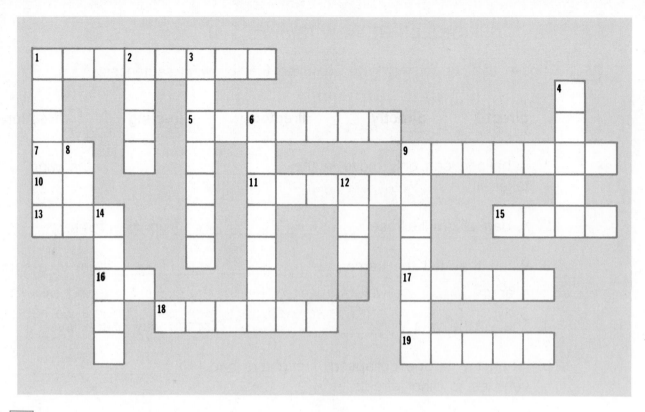

B Choose words from the word box to complete the crossword puzzle.

___ **Word Box** ___

amaze	excite	net	on
bridge	fled	scene	go
capture	forge	steward	ill
cellars	inspect	moat	
dismount	tower	unicorn	
dragon	we	one	

Across

1. get off
5. look at carefully
7. to leave
9. to catch
10. opposite of *off*
11. to cause strong feeling
13. a fish catcher
15. got away fast
16. us
17. to surprise
18. something to help you cross deep water
19. location

Down

1. imaginary beast
2. ditch filled with water
3. animal never captured by humans
4. furnace for melting iron
6. one who takes care of castle lands
8. a number
9. basements
12. sick
14. tall, narrow building

38

C The topic sentence of a paragraph is not always the first sentence. It can be found anywhere in a paragraph. Read the following paragraphs. Underline the topic sentence in each.

1.  A saddle is a seat used by a person riding on a horse. The saddle is placed on the animal's back. A strap from the saddle fastens under the horse's body. It keeps the saddle from slipping off. The stirrups hang down from it. The rider's feet go in the stirrups. Most saddles are made of leather.

2. We left home early, but the car wouldn't start. While we were walking to the bus, a dog ran by and grabbed my notebook. We stopped in a restaurant to alert the police about the run-away dog. We had pancakes and orange juice while we waited. Finally, the police came and asked us a million questions. A police car was bringing me to school but we had to stop to fix a flat tire. That's why I'm two hours late for school, teacher.

3. The trees in the neighborhood were bright with color. Red, yellow, orange, and brown replaced the green of summer. Slowly the days became shorter. Autumn was bringing its many changes. At last the trees were becoming bare. At the same time, the weather was getting colder.

4. Sometimes, sailors landed on islands in the Pacific Ocean to get fresh water and food. One of their favorite foods was the fresh meat of the large turtles. They killed, cooked, and ate them on the islands. When they went back to their ships, they took live turtles with them so they would always have fresh meat. They would kill a turtle anytime the cook wanted to prepare a fresh meat dish.

D Sometimes the main idea of a paragraph is understood but not stated. Under the following paragraph, write the main idea. It is not directly stated in the paragraph, but it can be clearly understood.

Matilda and Thomas had to awaken early to do their chores. They fed the chickens first. Then they collected the eggs. Cleaning their room was the next task. Then they went out to the well to bring in pails of water. Father had already started a fire in the fireplace. Last of all, the children cleaned the oil lamps and refilled them. The whole family was proud of those lamps, so Matilda and Thomas were very careful. Grandma had their lunch buckets ready. Mother gave them each bread and cornmeal mush, which they ate in a hurry. Then they rushed off to school.

_____

_____

_____

E Study the following examples. Then label each example with the correct heading: **index**, **table of contents**, **dictionary**, **encyclopedia**, or **map**.

---

ocrea   **odic**

oc·ta·gon (ôk-tâ-gun) *n:* polygon having eight sides

oc·tag·o·nal (ôk-tâg-ô-nəl) *adj:* having eight angles and eight sides

---

1. _____

Sports, 215-219, 227-233, 307, 340-348;
  bicycling, 230, 342;
  fishing, 340, 346-348;
  hiking, 228-231, 345;
  karate, 340-342;
  skating, 347;
  swimming, 342-344, 348

---

2. _____   3. _____

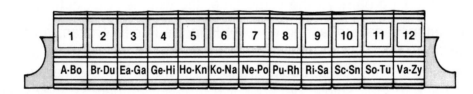

4. _____

What Is a Spider?
  What Spiders Look Like 6
  Parts of a Spider's Body .15

Spider Homes
  Building Nests and Webs 23
  Trapping Food. 39

---

5. _____

6. In which of these would you look to see how many pages a certain book has about the Arabian Sea?

_____   _____

7. In which of these would you look to learn how to pronounce *alopecia*?

_____

8. In which of these would you look to find the closest large city to the small town of Middletown, New York? _____

Here is part of the index from a book. See if you remember how to locate information in an index. Answer the following questions.

Motion pictures, 4, 15-50;
   acting schools, 16, 19;
   cartoons, 24-33;
   Disney, Walt, 28-30;
   Hollywood, 20, 34, 42, *photo*, 35;
   museums, 17, 18, 21-23;
      costumes, 45;
      locations, 43;
      stage sets, 46-50
Music, 3, 65-154;
   African, 65-75, 91;
   American, 100, 112-117;
   Chinese, 96-98;
   Indian, 142, 145, 147-149;

   instruments, 70, 81-129;
      cymbals, 71-75;
      drums, 70, 76-79, 92-96;
      guitar, 81-85, 114, 116-118;
      piano, 118, 127-129;
   Japanese, 150, 153, 154
Television, 6, 200-252;
   advertising, 202, 230-239;
   cameras, 220-227;
   educational, 210, 218;
   electronic games, 241-248, 250-252;
   taping, 239, 249-251;
   use of satellites, 200, 201

1. On what pages could you look to find out if Walt Disney is still living?

   _____

2. How many subtopics are given for television? _____

3. Would this book give you any information about a trumpet? _____

4. What page would help you see what Hollywood looks like? _____

5. How many pages could you check to find out how satellites help you see television programs? _____

6. Is there any information in this book that tells you how to buy a television set? _____

7. Which would be the best page to start to read about Indian music?

   _____

8. Are there more pages on Chinese music than on Japanese music?

   _____

9. Under the subtopic, *instruments*, which ones are discussed?

   _____

10. If the author had included Greek music in the book, where would this subtopic appear? _____

Choose the correct effect for each cause. Circle it.

1. Because Dad won the tickets,
    a. the Brents went to West Virginia.
    b. his name was announced at the game.
    c. the family went to California.

2. Because there was no electricity,
    a. people used flashlights and candles.
    b. automobiles could not start.
    c. batteries did not work.

3. Because the Brents went by plane,
    a. one bag was lost.
    b. they flew with the baseball team.
    c. they rented a car to get around.

4. Because the earthquake occurred,
    a. the game started early.
    b. some games were canceled.
    c. no tickets were honored.

H Choose the correct cause for each effect. Write the letter in the sentence.

Causes
a. Because Icarus flew too near the sun,
b. Because scientists wanted to know how strong earthquakes were,
c. Because birds fly fast and easily,
d. Because huge plates under the earth collided,
e. Because the Brents took a plane to California,
f. Because hydrogen is lighter than air,

---

1. _____, they made the Richter Scale.

2. _____, people wanted to imitate them.

3. _____, the wax on his feathers melted.

4. _____, the light towers swayed and trembled.

5. _____, the balloons soared into the sky.

5

My name is Donna. I don't mean to brag, but I am a detective. You can be a detective, too. Just watch carefully, listen when people talk to you, and think.

This case started last Monday. Mrs. Jordan kept Liz after school to ask her to do something. A new girl would be entering our class the next day. Our teacher wanted Liz to show the new student around. Liz was asked to make her feel at home in a strange place.

On the way to school Tuesday morning, Liz said, "I'll tell you a secret. Mrs. Jordan has a special reason this time for asking me to help the new girl. Her name is Joanne Smart."

"Don't say another word!" I interrupted. "Anyone with the last name of Smart is going to get a lot of teasing and jokes about it! Mrs. Jordan wants you to stop the kids from making fun of her."

"There's Donna acting like a detective again!" exclaimed Glenn, Liz's older brother.

Liz nodded her head. "You're right, Donna," she said. "I'm to make sure that no one hurts Joanne's feelings."

My brother, Nicky, started to giggle as we got to the school playground. "It'll be easy to find Joanne! She's the one with the big brain!"

Glenn, Liz, and I scolded Nicky until he promised to be quiet. Then I gazed around the school grounds, trying to find which one in the mob of noisy students was Joanne.

I looked and thought, "If I were new, where would I stay until the bell rang? The door! I'd hang around the door sizing up the kids."

We moved closer to the door. I spotted a girl.

"There she is!" I said. "I'll bet that's Joanne."

"Oh, come on!" moaned Glenn. "The great detective strikes again. How do you know that's Joanne?"

I explained, "She's got an adult with her. It's probably her father bringing her for the first day. She's got that I-dare-you-to-make-fun-of-my-name look in her eyes. She is nervous, but she's not afraid. Because her name is Smart, she has learned to protect herself."

"Hey, Donna!" laughed Glenn. "I dare you to tell us more about that girl. A smart detective like you should be able to give us her whole biography!"

Whenever people say things like that to me, I'm ready to go on the warpath. They could be detectives, too. All they have to do is listen carefully, watch, and think.

I watched the girl for a while longer. Then I saw some things. I thought about them.

"Don't laugh at me," I said, "because I might be all wrong. But here is what I think. That girl, whoever she is, does a lot of writing. She probably always has her homework done. She writes with her left hand. Just a short time ago, she probably had a broken leg. She is outdoors often when it is dark. It might be that she delivers newspapers."

"Wow!" said Nicky. "You are really out on a limb now! How can you know all that?"

"I'm sure of some of it," I answered.

"We'll find out in class," said Liz just as the bell rang.

I was right about one thing. The girl we had been watching was in our class. Mrs. Jordan introduced her to Liz as Joanne. Liz showed Joanne the lockers, the lavatory, the cafeteria, and the library. She let her meet the other students.

By lunchtime, I thought Joanne felt comfortable enough to answer a few questions for Liz.

Liz told her what I had said.

Joanne's eyes grew wide. "How did you know? It's all true!"

"Anyone can tell," I said, and then explained how.

"People who write a lot get a bump on the middle finger bone where they hold a pencil. Joanne's bump is on her left hand.

"Now look at her blue and yellow tennis shoes," I said. "The right one looks like new. The left one is faded and worn. How can that be? The right one has not been worn much. Joanne could only have walked about with one shoe if she had a walking cast on the other foot. That could mean her right leg was broken. Now that it has healed, Joanne is wearing both shoes." The other students nodded in agreement.

I went on. "See the stripes on Joanne's jacket. They are the kind that shine in the dark. That means she is out walking, running, or riding her bike at night. There is a black spot on the jacket. It looks like newsprint, which comes off on everything. It could come from newspapers that Joanne delivers. Putting the spot and the stripes together might mean that Joanne is out in the dark delivering morning papers."

"You're quite a detective, Donna!" Joanne exclaimed.

The rest of the students were amazed. They got so excited about Joanne that they forgot to ask her last name. By the time they found out, she was too well-liked and respected for much teasing. Joanne often thanked me for helping her get accepted so quickly by her new classmates.

Underline the correct answer to each question.

1. Why was Mrs. Jordan worried about Joanne?

   a. She thought the other children would make fun of her.
   b. She thought Joanne would be nasty to the other students.
   c. She thought Joanne would be too shy to speak to the other students.
   d. She thought Joanne would have trouble walking with her broken leg.

2. Why do you think Mrs. Jordan asked Liz to take care of Joanne?
   a. The story did not say.
   b. Liz was older than the others.
   c. Liz lived next door to Joanne.
   d. Liz could get along well with other people.

3. What didn't Liz do for Joanne the first day?
   a. Liz taught Joanne to find her way around the school.
   b. Liz helped Joanne to feel at home in a new school.
   c. Liz taught Joanne the reading work.
   d. Liz introduced Joanne to some of the students.

4. When do you think Mrs. Jordan asked Liz to take care of Joanne?
   a. Tuesday afternoon   b. Friday morning
   c. before Tuesday   d. after Tuesday

5. Why did Nicky say he was going to look for a big brain?
   a. He was looking for materials for his science class.
   b. He was making fun of Joanne's name.
   c. He was interested in ocean life.
   d. Mother had sent him to the store for some books.

6. How do you think Joanne felt as she stood by the school door?
   a. proud and happy
   b. calm and pleased with herself
   c. jealous and angry
   d. frightened and excited

7. Why was Donna sure Joanne had had a broken leg?
   a. She was walking with crutches.
   b. There was a cast on her leg.
   c. They heard Joanne's father say, "Don't break the other leg."
   d. One shoe looked worn, but the other looked new.

46

8. How did Joanne break a leg?

   a. She fell off her bike while delivering papers.

   b. She was hit by a truck driver who did not see her in the dark.

   c. She fell down the steps in her other school.

   d. The story did not say.

9. How do we know Joanne followed safety rules?

   a. She never crossed the street without looking in both directions first.

   b. She always wore a jacket with stripes that shine in the dark to deliver papers.

   c. She never ran from between parked cars.

   d. She always went to the corner to cross the street even if it took her out of her way.

10. Why didn't Joanne need much protection?

   a. She had taken many karate lessons.

   b. She was older and taller than the other students.

   c. After years of teasing, she knew how to defend herself.

   d. Mr. and Mrs. Smart stayed in school with Joanne to stop the teasing.

11. After the class learned Joanne's name, why didn't they tease her much?

   a. Most of the students liked and respected her.

   b. The children were afraid of her.

   c. The students were afraid of her father.

   d. The students were afraid of Mrs. Jordan.

12. What was the story mainly about?

   a. how Mrs. Jordan, Glenn, Nicky, and Liz made Joanne feel at home

   b. how a teacher and two girls helped a new student feel at home

   c. how Joanne's father helped her when it was necessary

   d. a boy who was pleasant, dependable, quiet, and clever

13. What kind of a teacher was Mrs. Jordan?

   a. a stern, hard teacher

   b. a new teacher

   c. an understanding and caring teacher

   d. a polite teacher

14. What would be a good title for this story?

   a. Donna Brags Again

   b. Help for a New Student

   c. A Job Before School

   d. School Children Are Cruel

What are these expressions and words really saying? Match column **A** with column **B**. Write the letter of the correct meaning from column **B** next to each sentence in column **A**.

Column A

_____ 1. Liz was *the answer to any teacher's dream*.

_____ 2. Donna was always *sizing up others*.

_____ 3. I was *on the warpath*.

_____ 4. Liz always *mothered* the new classmates.

_____ 5. Donna had put herself *out on a limb again*.

_____ 6. Nicky *interrupted* Liz's story several times.

_____ 7. Please come straight home. *Don't hang around* the playground

_____ 8. The whole class was *amazed* at Donna's work.

_____ 9. Joanne began to *feel at home*.

_____ 10. Liz's eyes *grew wide*.

_____ 11. Joanne could not *find her way around*.

_____ 12. No one should *hurt her feelings*.

_____ 13. I *spotted* someone.

_____ 14. Tell us his *biography*.

Column B

a. took good care of; guarded

b. stared

c. very surprised

d. noticed

e. absent

f. ready to fight

g. know where everything was

h. broke into

i. life story

j. the kind of child an adult could depend on

k. stay longer than is necessary

l. studying people to try to understand them better

m. in a spot from which it would be hard to escape without embarrassment

n. was comfortable

o. insult her

Liz's older brother, Glenn, is in the eighth grade. He is a reporter for the school newspaper. Below are some articles that Glenn has written. Each one needs a headline. Help Glenn. Using the box below as a guide, write a headline for each story. One is done for you.

> 1. The headline should tell the main idea or topic of the article.
> 2. The headline is not written in sentence form. It is written as a phrase.
> 3. The important words in a headline start with capital letters.

1.
Boy Rewarded for Helping Cat

Hugh Baldwin has proved that a kind heart can pay off. On November 3, Hugh found a cat lying in the street. The animal had a broken leg. Hugh was on his way to school, but he stopped to help.

He got some water for the cat. Then he sat by the cat waiting for passersby. At last, Mrs. Belle Simkins of 3982 Bow Avenue saw them and stopped.

Mrs. Simkins and Hugh took the cat to the veterinarian. There it was treated. While Hugh went on to school, the owner was located. Hugh received a reward of $25 from the cat's grateful master.

2. _____

One science class, in Room 603, has been raising tadpoles for the last three weeks. Lea Tolson, a fifth grader, found the frog eggs in a pond on Edgewood Avenue. The class has watched, fed, and learned from the tadpoles as they've hatched from the eggs.

(continued on page 50)

For the Thanksgiving holiday, Lea offered to take the tadpoles home. Somehow, in her rush to start the vacation, she forgot them in the classroom.

The class was upset upon returning the following Monday morning to discover that most of the tadpoles had turned into frogs and gone their own ways.

That day, science class changed into a frog hunt.
It is reported that the creatures were found jumping about in the halls, the sinks, the heating plant, the waste cans, and the classrooms of the whole first floor. Dr. Mead, our principal, leaped fast to capture one frog in his desk drawer and another by his telephone. Maybe the frog was planning to order some flies for lunch.

3. _____

    _____

Fifth-grade students at Crest School are displaying what they made in art class this term. The art show will be held on June 7 in the auditorium. The Parent-Teacher Association will be meeting that night. Many parents are expected to come to view the masterpieces of their children. The art teachers have put on a beautiful show. The colorful pottery is gathering praise from all who have seen it arranged on one side of the room. Beautiful watercolor paintings are displayed on the stage. Puppets, weavings, and needlework are placed near the windows. Cutouts and dioramas are by the door.

Dr. Mead, the principal, has given permission for students to view the art every day after school from June 8 to June 23.

D Read these sentences. Most of them belong in one paragraph. Label the sentence that tells the main idea with the letters **M.I.** Place **D** next to the other sentences that are details supporting the main idea. Two sentences do not help the main idea or topic, so they do not belong. Label them **X**.

_____ 1. Joanne rides her bike from door to door delivering papers early each morning.

_____ 2. Joanne likes to read the comics in the morning paper.

_____ 3. People complain if Joanne is careless and the paper lands in the bushes or on the roof. So Joanne puts each paper where it should go.

_____ 4. Joanne must go out every two weeks to collect money for the papers she has delivered.

_____ 5. Joanne does not have an easy job.

_____ 6. Newspapers give us much information on many topics.

_____ 7. At sunrise, a truck leaves a pile of papers at Joanne's door. She must fold them. They must be put into plastic bags on rainy days.

_____ 8. Because some of her customers live on the second floor, Joanne walks up many steps each day.

Early Sunday morning, Loretta was awakened by the sound of a terrible crash on the steep hill near her grandmother's house.

"Guess what, Gran?" she said. "In our English class, we are putting out a school newspaper. Do you think I should go see what happened? It might be an interesting article for the newspaper."

"I think it sounded like a car accident," Grandmother remarked, "and it is the kind of news that papers will print."

All that evening, Loretta struggled to write a newspaper article. She wrote a headline that she felt gave a good idea of the contents of the story.

The next day on the school bus she read to some of her classmates what she had written.

Valerie exclaimed, "That's a great story! I enjoyed the excitement!"

"I felt as if I were right there in the pileup," said Tyrone.

Loretta could hardly wait for the English lesson to begin. She raised her hand immediately to show Mr. Fedder, the teacher, her article. While the rest of the group worked on their projects, he studied it.

Loretta was bubbling over. "I hope you think it is good enough for our class newspaper, Mr. Fedder."

Mr. Fedder praised the fact that there were no spelling errors.

"The sentences all start with capital letters and end with periods," he complimented. "Good work, Loretta."

But then the girl was disappointed.

"You will have to make a few important changes," the teacher suggested. "This is going to be a newspaper story. You forgot what all newspaper stories should have."

Loretta studied her work. She read it again and again.

Ice Causes Pileup When Truck Overturns

An unexpected drop in temperature after midnight caused ice to form on many roads. On steep Fleming Hill, several cars were stuck. As more cars slid down the hill, there was a giant pileup. The police should have closed the street, but they did not.

At 3:10 a.m., Lois Fant, driver of a large truck, started down the hill. Trying to stop the truck did not help. It joined the rest of the pileup, ending overturned across the road. That, finally, closed the road to traffic. It probably prevented even more accidents. The load on the truck, 8,500 cases of Foamy Soap, covered the road.

Then Loretta said, "Newspapers print all the facts. I have plenty of facts here."

"Indeed you do," agreed Mr. Fedder. "You have facts. But you have something else, too."

Then Loretta knew.

"Some of the article is my own opinion!" she said, discovering the truth. "Reporters should only tell facts!"

"Good thinking!" praised Mr. Fedder. "But I believe our class may need some work on telling the difference between facts and opinions."

The whole group discussed the differences for awhile. They discovered:

1. A *fact* is a true piece of information. You must be able to prove your facts by showing where you found the information.

2. An *opinion* is what someone thinks about a topic. An opinion is not always a fact. This is because most people have different opinions about the same topic.

3. An opinion may be true, but it is still an opinion.

A Reread the newspaper article. Find the sentences that are opinions rather than facts. Write them here.

_____

_____

_____

_____

_____

_____

The next day, Mr. Fedder had a big box in class. It was wrapped in beautiful yellow and silver paper. The bow on top was dotted with small, yellow stars. The children gathered around it.

"Who gave you a present?" they asked.

"It's a gift for you, not for me!" laughed their teacher. "In this box are some very interesting topics. Each of you will pick one and look up information on it. When you have found out everything you can, write fifteen facts about your topic. Notice that I said facts. Please do not write opinions. The students who write few or no opinions will each find a surprise in this gift box three weeks from today!"

In great excitement, one at a time, the students went up to the box, closed their eyes, and fished out a slip of paper! Then the shouting began.

The topics were things about which they had never heard! The students thought Mr. Fedder was fooling them.

"No, they're real!" he said. "If you knew what these things were, you would be able to write the facts without searching. The hunt is half the fun!"

Norman shouted, "Mine is something called *Ixora*!"

"That's all right," said Mr. Fedder. "Pick another."

In went Norman's hand again. Out it came! "*Kittiwake*!" he called. "That's worse than *Ixora*!"

"Do you want to try again?" inquired Mr. Fedder.

Norman shook his head. "I'd probably get one even worse."

For several days, the students hunted in dictionaries, in encyclopedias, and in many indexes of books. They used all their study skills. They read and thought. Then they started to put down facts.

On the following pages are some of the papers the students wrote. Now pretend you are Mr. Fedder. Mark the papers. Make a ✔ by every fact. Make an **X** by every opinion. Count all the checks. Write the number at the top of the paper. If the student gets a score of 12 or more, she or he will get a surprise from the box.

The Kakapo

The kakapo is a very noisy bird of the parrot family. It is flightless, which means that it is unable to fly. The kakapo runs about on the ground. It has not flown for so many centuries that its wing muscles are tiny and weak.

The home of the kakapo is in a burrow under the ground. The birds move into holes that have been left by other animals. Throughout the day, the kakapos hide in their burrows.

As soon as it is dark, they crawl out, noisy and hungry. Their search for food continues until dawn. Their favorite food is the nectar of flowers. Kakapos locate the blossoms in the darkness by following the odor of the nectar.

Their brown feathers are arranged in a light and dark pattern that appears to be in stripes. This makes them very difficult to spot in the moonlight and shadows. Kakapos have beaks just like other parrots. However, around their bills are feathers that look like whiskers.

Very few kakapos remain. They are almost extinct because they taste good and people have killed them for food. As more cities have spread out in the country, the animals that live with people have attacked the kakapos in their neighborhoods. The parrots are easy prey because they are unable to fly away.

Carmen Castillo _____

Kakapos

1. Kakapos are parrots that cannot fly.
2. They are almost extinct because humans like to eat them.
3. People should eat only vegetables to stop killing off many different kinds of animals.
4. Kakapos come out only at night to hunt for nectar in the flowers.
5. Rats, cats, and dogs destroy kakapos.
6. Kakapos live in burrows that other animals have dug.
7. The wing muscles of kakapos have gotten weak because they are not used.
8. Kakapos are very cute birds.
9. Human beings find it easy to kill kakapos. They could capture them instead and keep them as pets. That would keep many more kakapos alive, and they would not become extinct.
10. Kakapos find nectar in flowers at night by using their noses. They track the smell of the nectar until they find it.
11. Kakapos are noisy.
12. Kakapos hide in the daytime.
13. Kakapos have hooked beaks like parrots.
14. The striped, brown feathers make kakapos difficult to see at night.
15. Kakapos return to their burrows by sunrise.

The Guacharo

In South America, in the mountain caves along the coast lives a bird called gaucharo or oilbird. It is found in Peru, Ecuador, Colombia, Venezuela, and Trinidad. For centuries the fat of the young guacharos has been boiled. From the boiled fat, humans obtain a clear, yellow, odorless oil. The people use it to cook and for lighting for their homes.

The guacharo spends most of its life in darkness. It has large, blue eyes, short legs, weak feet, and a strong, yellow, hooked bill. When it spreads its wings, they stretch out to 36 inches. The color of the guacharo is reddish-brown, spotted with black and white. Around its mouth are long, stiff bristles.

As it flies around in the dark cave, the guacharo gives off clicking sounds. Echoes come back to the guacharo. This helps the bird avoid bumping into anything that is in the way.

Deep in the caves, the guacharo builds its nest on ledges. In the saucer-shaped nest are laid two, three, or four white eggs. Both parents take turns sitting on the eggs until they hatch.

At night the guacharo leaves the cave to get food. It eats the oily fruits of palms and laurels. It is the only fruit-eating bird in the world that flies at night.

Gwen King _____

Guacharos

1. Guacharos are birds found in South America.

2. People kill Guacharos to get the fat they need for oil.

3. After removing the fat, people probably eat the guacharo because it looks good enough to eat.

4. The guacharo builds a saucer-shaped nest.

5. The guacharo likes to live in dark places, such as caves.

6. If there were enough guacharo birds in the world, the guacharo oil could be used in the motors of cars, trucks, ships and planes.

7. The guacharo is an attractive bird with beautiful, blue eyes,

8. People can only see the birds outside of caves during the night.

9. All echoes come from sounds made by the guacharos.

10. The guacharo lays two to four white eggs.

11. The mother and father guacharos help take care of the eggs.

12. The guacharo likes to eat oily fruit.

13. The guacharo's wings can spread out to 36 inches.

14. The eyes of a guacharo are blue.

15. **Some** people use the oil from a guacharo to light their homes.

Quack Grass

In the United States and Canada, one of the worst plant pests is called quack grass. It also has several other names, such as devil's grass, witch grass, and quick grass. This weed was brought here from Europe, and it has been spreading rapidly ever since.

Quack grass is tall. It can be two, three, or four feet high. Under the ground lies the most serious cause of trouble. The roots form rhizomes. Rhizomes are strong, tough, horizontal roots that fan out in all directions. Leaves grow right on the rhizomes, come out above the soil and sprout new plants. In this way new patches of quack grass appear in different areas.

At the same time, the plant above the ground produces seeds. The seeds are spread by the breezes, by animals, and by birds. Many of the seeds start new quack grass plants, too. Once it forms, the quack grass chokes all the other neighboring plants. Farm crops and gardens have been destroyed by quack grass pushing them out.

It is difficult to get rid of quack grass. Digging it out does not work. If even a tiny part of the rhizome is left, it begins to sprout new plants. Poisons can kill it, but they can destroy other plantings, too.

Quack grass can be useful. Goats, sheep, and cattle are able to graze on it. On hills and on the banks of streams and rivers, the tough rhizomes of quack grass hold the soil more firmly in place to prevent it from washing away.

Alexander Lewis

Quack Grass

1. Quack grass is also called witchgrass.
2. All people hate quack grass.
3. The rhizomes are the roots of the quack grass.
4. The rhizomes spread horizontally under the ground. In this way, quack grass can pop out in different areas.
5. The rhizomes are hard and tough.
6. If the rhizomes are cut out, every bit of them must be removed.
7. If any part of the root is left in the ground, it can sprout new plants.
8. Cattle can use quack grass as food.
9. By spending much money on weed killers, the governments of the United States and Canada could destroy every bit of the quack grass. This would be good for farmers.
10. Quack grass is useful to hold the soil in place in hilly areas.
11. Quack grass is ugly.
12. Quack grass is a tall plant.
13. Quack grass keeps nearby plants from getting water and food from the soil. It chokes them out in this way.
14. Quack plants have stems, leaves and seeds.
15. The seeds are scattered by the wind. They start new plants.

C Choose a word from the word box below to complete each sentence.

```
─────────────── Word Box ───────────────
  prevent            immediately          rhizomes
  approach           opinions             sprout
  compliment         praise               article
  rely               disappoint           errors
  attractive         remark               steep
```

1. A hill that is hard to climb is _____.

2. Mistakes are _____.

3. To say something is to _____.

4. Your thoughts about a subject are _____.

5. To come near is to _____.

6. To praise is to _____.

7. When a seed begins to grow, it starts to _____.

8. Tough, strong, horizontal roots are _____.

9. To stop from happening is to _____.

10. To break a promise is to _____.

11. To do something right away is to do it _____.

12. To depend on is to _____.

13. A pretty scene is _____.

14. A baby plant is a _____.

15. A story written for a newspaper is an _____.

7

An **outline** is a way to study a story or an article and write its information in a shorter form. It is a good way to write down what you have read in your own words without copying many pages of information. Outlines can help you remember what you have read and learned.

Read this outline about a popular product. Then answer the questions in exercise A.

A Popular Product—Chewing Gum

I. Used by ancient Greeks
   A. Chewed resin of mastic tree
   B. Gave us our word *masticate*,
      meaning **chew**

II. Used by Wampanoag Indians in North America
   A. Chewed pieces of resin or sap from spruce trees
      1. Were tough to chew
      2. Tasted bad
   B. Introduced to the Pilgrims in 1600s

III. Began to spread in 1800s
   A. Introduction of spruce gum made with paraffin
      1. Introduced in Maine by John Curtis
      2. Introduced in 1848
   B. Discovery of Osage Indians' chewing gum
      1. Discovered by pioneers settling the West
      2. Made of chicle, the sap of the Mexican sapodilla tree

C. Invention of chicle chewing gum with many flavors
   1. Invented by Thomas Adams
   2. First sold in the United States in 1870
   3. Made in popular flavors
      a. Licorice
      b. Cinnamon
      c. Clove
      d. Peppermint
      e. Spearmint

IV. Used throughout world in 1900s
  A. Growth of Wrigley Company
    1. Gum used across the United States
    2. Sold in stores
    3. Sold in vending machines
  B. Spread to other countries and continents
    1. Australia
    2. New Zealand
    3. Canada
    4. Europe
    5. Asia
  C. Growing sapodilla trees in Mexico
    1. Growing a tree for 60 or 70 years before getting chicle from it
    2. Collecting sap from a cut in the trunk of the sapodilla tree
    3. Selling sap or chicle to gum companies all over the world
    4. Becoming the main chicle exporting country in the world
  D. Trying to develop synthetic products to make chewing gum
  E. Invention of bubble gum in 1933
  F. Giving away baseball cards with chewing gum
  G. Invention of sugarless gum in 1940

V. Further Developments
  A. Will not cause tooth decay
  B. Is better for the health of people

Underline the correct answer to each question.

1. What kind of information is in this outline?
   a. how bubble gum is made
   b. the ingredients in a stick of gum
   c. the history of chewing gum
   d. the most popular gum flavor

2. What is known about the use of gum in ancient times?
   a. It is mentioned in the Bible.
   b. It was discovered by the Romans.
   c. It was used in ancient Egypt.
   d. It was used in ancient Greece.

3. What is the title of the outline?
   a. Chewing Gum   b. The History of Invention
   c. A Popular Product—Chewing Gum   d. The World's Greatest Invention

4. The **main topics** of an outline are shown by the use of Roman numbers. How many main topics are in this outline?
   a. six   b. fifteen   c. fourteen   d. five

5. The **subtopics** are under the main topics. They are shown by the use of capital letters. How many subtopics are under the third main topic?
   a. five   b. two   c. four   d. three

6. When did chewing gum begin to be used all over the world?
   a. in the 1800s   b. in the 1900s
   c. in the 1600s   d. during ancient times

7. Chicle is what part of the sapodilla tree?
   a. the bark   b. the sap
   c. the leaf   d. It is not part of it.

8. What did the ancient Greeks chew?
   a. chicle   b. sap from the sapodilla tree
   c. resin from the spruce tree   d. resin from the mastic tree

9. Why do you think the chewing gum makers are trying to make gum from synthetic materials?
   a. Spruce trees are becoming scarce in the world.
   b. There is a disease that is destroying many chicle trees in the world.
   c. The sapodilla trees in Mexico have become too old.
   d. It takes a long time for sapodilla trees to produce enough chicle.

B Outlines are one way to write down information in a shorter form. **Graphs** are another means of doing this. Graphs compare things. A graph shows a clear picture and is easy to understand. Here is some more information about chewing gum. It is shown on a **circle graph**. Read the graph and answer the questions.

Ingredients in Modern Chewing Gum

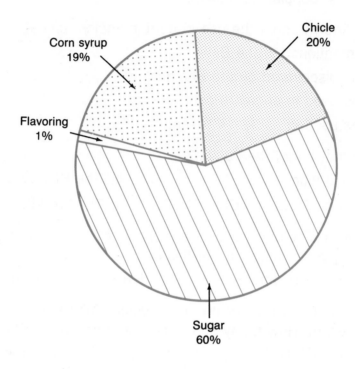

1. How many ingredients are in most modern chewing gums? _____

2. Name all the ingredients used in chewing gum.

   _____

3. Which ingredient is used most in making chewing gum?_____

4. Which ingredient is used least in making chewing gum?_____

5. Which ingredients are used in almost the same amount in making chewing gum?

   _____

6. Is there more chicle or more corn syrup in gum? _____

7. Is there less chicle or less sugar in gum? _____

8. What information does this circle graph show?

   _____

C Below is a **bar graph**. Read the information on it and answer the questions.

Favorite Gum Flavors Among School Children

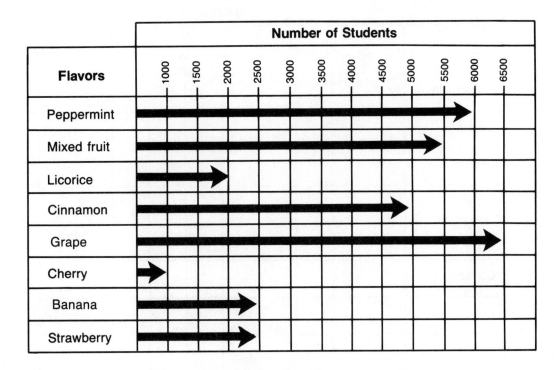

1. Which was the least popular flavor among the children?

   _____

2. Which was the most popular flavor? _____

3. Which two flavors were equally popular with the children?

   _____

4. About how many children chose cinnamon? _____

5. About how many children chose peppermint? _____

6. Did the children like mixed fruit or banana gum better?

   _____

7. Which was more popular, cinnamon or grape gum?

   _____

8. What information does this bar graph show?

   _____

   _____

Read the bar graph and answer the following questions.

How Much Sugarless Gum Was Chewed in the World in 1980

	NUMBER OF PEOPLE											
	2500	3000	3500	4000	4500	5000	5500	6000	6500	7000	7500	8000
United States												
Germany												
Mexico												
France												
Russia												
Canada												
England												
Sweden												

1. How many people in England chewed sugarless gum? _____

2. Which country had the least number of sugarless gum chewers?

   _____

3. Which country used more sugarless gum, Sweden or Germany?

   _____

4. How many people in Mexico chewed sugarless gum? _____

5. How many more people chewed sugarless gum in France than in Sweden?

   _____

6. What countries chewed the same amount?

   _____

7. How many fewer Canadians chewed sugarless gum than Americans?

   _____

8. What information does this bar graph show?

   _____

After you have located information, you usually have a jumble of facts. Most good students put these facts in an outline under different topics. Once the information is outlined, it is easy to find any fact quickly.

An outline is a shorter way of writing and remembering information. Only main ideas and important details are included. Here is a form that should be used to outline material.

_____ (The **title** explains the main idea of the whole article.)

(This is the **main topic** of the paragraph. Main ideas use Roman numerals.)
  I.
    A.
    B. (These are the supporting details of the same paragraph. They are called **subtopics**.)
    C.
    D.

(This is the main topic of the second paragraph.)
  II.
    A.
    B. (Subtopics use capital letters.)
    C.

(This is the main topic of the third paragraph.)
  III.
    A.
    B.
    C.
      1. (These are additional **details** for subtopic C. These use Arabic numbers.)
      2.

A Read the following article. Think of how you would outline the information. Then complete the outline after the article.

The Linnaea, or twinflower, is a beautiful plant. It is an evergreen, so it does not lose its leaves in the winter. It has long, woody stems. The leaves are round, and the flowers are shaped like bells. They can be either pink or white. A sweet, pleasant odor is given off by the pretty blossoms.

The twinflower is found only in a few places. It grows in North America, in Sweden and Norway, and in some parts of Asia. It requires loose, damp soil.

It is easy to grow Linnaeas. Just cut off a section of the stem. Put it in some water. Wait a few days until roots form. Then plant it in some soft, fine soil. Water it often.

_____ (Title)

I. _____

    A. Is an evergreen
       1. Stays green all winter
       2. Does not lose its leaves in the cold
    B. Has long, woody stems
    C. Has round leaves
    D. Has bell-shaped flowers
    E. Has white or pink blossoms
    F. Gives off a sweet, pleasant odor

II. _____

    A. Grows in North America
    B. Grows in Norway and Sweden
    C. Grows in Asia
    D. Requires loose, damp soil

III. _____

    A. Cut off a part of the stem.
    B. Place in water.
    C. Wait for roots to grow.
    D. Plant in right place.
    E. Water often.

B Read this article. Then complete the outline with the information you have read.

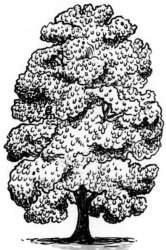

The tulip tree, or tulip poplar, is outstanding in appearance. It is the tallest broadleaf tree found in the eastern United States. It can grow two hundred feet high. Its trunk can be as wide as a car is long. The beautiful, yellow blossoms look like tulips. Its long-stemmed, smooth, graceful leaves are notched. The outer wood, or the bark, of the tree is white. The inner wood is a pretty shade of yellow.

The tulip poplar is found only in North America. The tree grows in the eastern United States from Maine to Florida. It also grows as far west as Arkansas. Since this tree is the state tree of Tennessee, Kentucky, and Indiana, it is found in these states, too.

The tulip tree has several uses. It produces hard wood that is very valuable. Expensive furniture is made from it. The tulip poplar is used to make beautiful baskets, boxes, and ornaments, too.

_____(Title)

I. Is outstanding in appearance _____

    A. _____

    B. _____

    C. _____

    D. _____

    E. _____

    F. _____

    G. _____

II. Is found only in North America _____

    A. _____

    B. _____

    C. Is the state tree of three states _____

        1. _____

        2. _____

        3. _____

III. Has several uses _____

    A. _____

    B. _____

    C. _____

    D. _____

Read this article about an odd animal. Prepare a complete outline from what you read. If you look back at the sample outlines, you will find it easy to write your own outline.

The tailorbird has unusual nesting habits. It starts to build a nest by putting two broad leaves together. It uses its sharp beak to stab holes in the edges of the leaves. Then it uses a spider web as thread to sew the leaves together. The nest it makes is like a sack with an open top. The tailorbird lines its nest to make the baby birds comfortable. To do this, it uses silky threads from plants, soft grass, or animal hairs. The nest is hidden in thick bushes. Two or three speckled eggs are laid in a nest.

The tailorbird looks unusual, too. It is only four to six inches long. Its bill is very thin and sharp. Its head is red. The back of the tailorbird is olive green, but its front is light gray. Its long tail sticks up straight in the air. Its voice is harsh and noisy.

Tailorbirds are found in few places. They will live only in areas that have been settled and cleared by people. They make homes in gardens and on farms. They can be seen in India, the East Indies, and the Philippine Islands.

I. _____

   A. _____

      1. _____

      2. _____

B. _____

C. _____

    1. _____

    2. _____

    3. _____

D. _____

E. _____

II. _____

A. _____

B. _____

C. _____

D. _____

E. _____

F. _____

III. _____

A. _____

B. _____

C. _____

D Study the outline below. Then label the parts marked by stars. Use the labels from the box.

a. Additional details for subtopics	b. Subtopics
c. Title	d. Main topic

The Brown Pelican

★1. _____

I. Where found
  A. On the warmer parts of the east and west coasts of the United States
  B. On the east and west coasts of Central America
  C. On the east and west coasts halfway down South America

★2. _____

II. Nesting habits

★3. _____

  A. Choosing of nesting site by males
  B. Finding a mate
  C. Searching for nest materials by males
    1. Sticks   4. Leaves
    2. Straw   5. Grass
    3. Reeds

★4. _____

  D. Building of nest by females

★5. _____

  E. Laying two or three eggs
  F. Sitting on eggs by both parents
  G. Shading of the naked chicks from the sun by both parents
  H. Feeding of babies by both parents

★6. _____

III. Fishing habits

★7. _____

  A. Catch fish in pouch under bill
  B. Catch fish under the water
  C. Catch many fish easily

★8. _____

Underline the correct answer to each question.

1. Why must pelican parents shade their babies?
   a. Baby pelican chicks will not eat when it is sunny.
   b. Baby pelicans are not covered with feathers.
   c. The parents must keep the rain off the babies.
   d. The eggs must be protected from wild animals.

2. How do tailorbirds sew their nests together?
   a. with needle and thread
   b. with their beaks and cotton thread
   c. with stones and animal hairs
   d. with their beaks and spider web threads

3. What is true about tailorbirds?
   a. They like to live in the crowded jungle.
   b. They live in the icy places of the North Pole.
   c. They live where people live.
   d. They live far away from human beings.

4. Where are tailorbirds found?
   a. South America   b. the United States
   c. India   d. Antarctica

5. What statement is true about the Linnaea?
   a. It keeps its leaves in winter.
   b. It loses its leaves in cold weather.
   c. It gives off a bad odor.
   d. It looks like a daisy.

6. For what is the tulip poplar used?
   a. Its flowers are used as food for humans.
   b. People eat its leaves.
   c. The roots are used in medicine.
   d. Its wood makes good furniture.

7. If a tailorbird is measured against a 12-inch ruler, what is true?
   a. It is longer than the ruler.   b. It is a yard long.
   c. It is shorter than the ruler.   d. It is about as long as the ruler.

8. How do pelicans catch fish?
   a. in their pouches   b. from fishermen's nets
   c. with their webbed feet   d. from fishermen's lines

F Write the correct word on the line to complete each sentence.

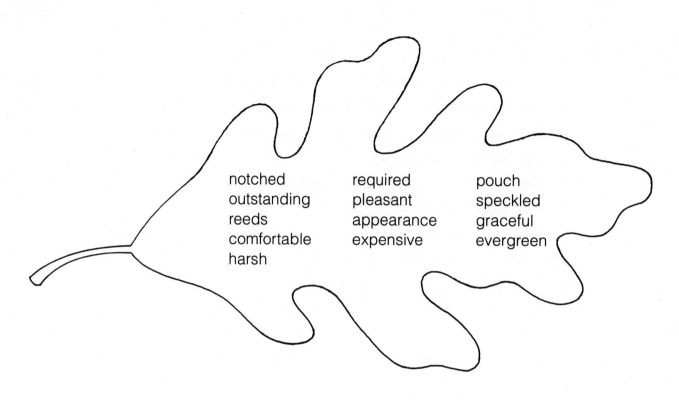

notched
outstanding
reeds
comfortable
harsh

required
pleasant
appearance
expensive

pouch
speckled
graceful
evergreen

1. To come out on a stage is to make an _____.

2. Something covered with small spots is _____.

3. If the sofa is soft and wide, it is probably _____.

4. To be a dancer, a person must be _____.

5. A friendly person is usually _____.

6. If boots cost a lot of money, they are _____.

7. A _____ is a kind of small bag.

8. Around most ponds, tall, slender _____ are to be found.

9. The noises that crows make are loud and _____.

10. Pines and spruces are called _____ trees.

11. If you have read the stories and know the definitions of all these words, you have done an _____ job.

12. The leaf in this picture is _____.

One Saturday Jay heard his mother say to his dad, "Let's go to see the puffins. Find out what time we can go there."

Mr. Lane made a telephone call. "This afternoon is a good time," he told his wife.

Jay was curious. He did not know anyone by the name of Puffin. "They must be new friends," he thought.

"Mom, do they have any children my age? I hope they have some electronic games," Jay said aloud.

Mrs. Lane laughed. "Puffins are not people. Look up the word in your encyclopedia. Find out what they are."

Using the indexing skills he learned in school, Jay found some information. After reading about puffins, Jay was anxious to see them. He also wanted to tell his friends about this unusual bird.

 Help Jay remember the important facts about puffins by making an outline with main topics, subtopics, and details under some of the subtopics. Complete the outline at the end of the article.

Puffins

Puffins are usually found in cold places along coasts. These seabirds live in the chilly Arctic waters that are part of the northern Atlantic and Pacific oceans. Great numbers of them are found in Iceland. Some also can be seen in Great Britain and in Maine.

The puffin is an odd-looking bird. The top part of its body is black. The underside and the cheeks are white. An adult puffin is about the same size as a young duck. On land, a puffin waddles around on large, red feet. Its head is unusually big for the size of its body. The head appears even larger because the puffin has a beak like a parrot's. This beak is covered with heavy skin plates. The plates are round in shape and colored red, yellow, and blue. They make the puffin a very colorful bird until the plates are lost after mating.

Puffins' beaks are helpful for fighting off enemies. Male puffins proudly display their bills to attract a mate. These birds show they love each other by rubbing beaks together. During nesting time the beak acts as a shovel to dig a small hole in a patch of soft earth on the rocks. An egg is laid in the hole. When carrying food to baby birds, the parents' beaks double as cups and spoons. A puffin's beak is a useful tool.

The puffins have interesting nesting habits. In the spring they move to rocky, bare land. A whole group bands together in one colony. Each pair finds a nest in a crack of a rock or a shallow hole. Only one white egg is laid in each nest. The egg is hatched in thirty days.

The puffin is an expert fisher. It catches different kinds of sea animals, such as smelt, herring, and shrimp. The puffin's wide beak can hold as many as ten fish to help feed the family.

_____ (Title)

I. _Where puffins are found_ _____

    A. _____

    B. _____

    C. _____

    D. _____

II. _____

    A. _____

    B. _____

    C. _____

    D. _____

E. _____

F. _____

    1. _____

    2. _____

    3. _____

    4. _____

III. _____

    A. _____

    B. _____

    C. _____

    D. _____

IV. _____

    A. _____

        1. _____

        2. _____

        3. _____

    B. _____

V. _____

    A. _____

    B. _____

B Below is a graph that shows a comparison. Gulls and puffins nest on the same rocky pieces of land in cold Arctic areas. The gulls often attack the puffins' nests to eat the eggs or the babies. People who study birds are afraid that in the future the gulls may kill off most of the puffins. A scientist has been keeping track of the number of puffins compared to the number of gulls in the Arctic regions. Study this **line graph**. You will find much information in a small space. Then answer the questions.

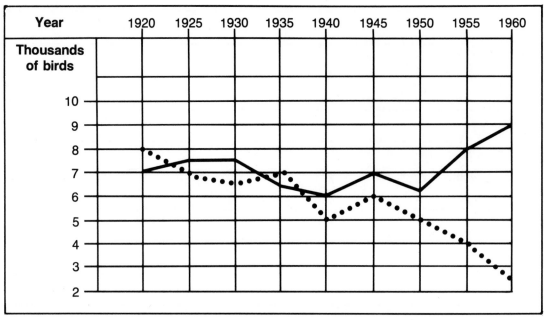

Puffins are represented by •••••••••.   Gulls are represented by ——————.

1. Which bird had the highest population in 1960? _____

2. When were there more puffins than gulls? Write all the years.

   _____

3. In what year was the population of gulls the lowest? _____

4. In what year was the puffin population the lowest? _____

5. In what years did the gull population remain the same?

   _____

6. In 1940, how many gulls were in the Arctic region? _____

7. In 1940, how many puffins were there? _____

8. How many gulls were there in 1950? _____

9. In 1940, how did the number of puffins compare to the number of gulls?

   _____

   _____

80

Study the **picture graph** below. Use the graph to answer the questions.

Different Species of Birds Found in North America, Europe, and India
United States (including Hawaii and Alaska)
Mexico
Canada
Europe
India

Each stands for 40 species.

1. One whole bird on the graph stands for _____ species.

2. Four whole birds on the graph stand for _____ species.

3. Half of a bird on the graph stands for _____ species.

4. Five and one-half birds on the graph stand for _____ species.

5. Where were most species found? _____

6. About how many were found there? _____

7. Where were the fewest species found? _____

8. How many species of birds were sighted in Mexico? _____

9. Five hundred and eighty species were found in _____ .

10. How many species of birds were counted in the United States? _____

11. How many more species were sighted in India than in Mexico? _____

12. How many fewer species of birds were sighted in the United States than

in India? _____

81

Here is a **circle graph** explaining which kinds of foods were most popular with puffins living in zoos in Great Britain. Study the graph and use it to answer the questions.

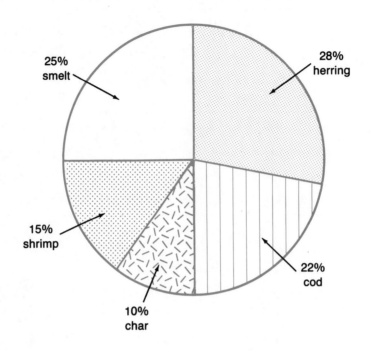

1. Which fish did puffins eat the least? _____

2. Which fish did puffins eat the most? _____

3. Did they eat more smelt or cod? _____

4. Which two foods together made up half of what the puffins ate?

   _____

5. Half of the circle equals _____ percent.

6. Did the puffins eat fewer shrimp or fewer char? _____

7. Did the puffins eat more shrimp or more cod? _____

8. Which was the second most popular food? _____

9. Which two foods together made up 25% of what the puffins ate?

   _____

10. Where did the people who made the graph study puffins?

   _____

SKILLS REVIEW (Stories 5-9)

 A Outlines help us put large amounts of reading material into fewer words. Outlines also help us remember important facts in articles. Study the following outline carefully and then answer the questions.

Poisonous Sea Animals

I. Crown of thorns starfish
   A. Attacks only to defend itself
   B. Uses spines
      1. Has spines covered with venom
      2. Causes painful puncture wounds with spines

II. Stingray
   A. Tries to avoid enemies
      1. Lies hidden in sand
      2. Moves away slowly
   B. Uses barbed stingers for defense
      1. Are hidden in tail
      2. Hurt enemy
      3. Push deep into enemies
      4. Leave venom in wounds

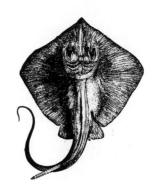

III. Stonefish
   A. Blends in with natural surroundings
      1. Found deep in soft sand, algae, or coral
      2. Stays hidden from human and sea enemies
   B. Attacks enemies
      1. Waits for enemies to come close
      2. Uses dorsal fin to jab enemies
   C. Has poisonous venom
      1. Makes victim unconscious
      2. May cause paralysis or death

1. How many subtopics are under main topic II? Circle the correct answer.

   a. four   b. three

   c. five   d. two

2. How many main topics are in the outline? Circle the correct answer.

   a. two   b. three

   c. four   d. five

3. What information is under main topic III, subtopic B, additional information number 2?

_____

4. What did you learn about the sea animals in this outline?

_____

_____

5. What can happen to a person if attacked by a stonefish?

_____

_____

6. How does the stingray avoid its enemy?

_____

7. What information is under main topic I, subtopic A?

_____

8. What kind of animal is the crown of thorns? _____

9. Where is the venom stored in the crown of thorns? _____

10. Where is the venom of the stingray stored? _____

11. What does the stonefish use to jab enemies? _____

12. Where are the stingray's barbed stingers hidden? _____

13. What information is under main topic II, subtopic B?

_____

14. What information is under main topic III, subtopic C, additional information 2?

_____

B Choose words from the box to complete the crossword puzzle.

_____ Word Box _____

amazed	dependable	masticate	quit	sprout
ancient	disappointed	midrib	relief	squirm
cap	fizz	popular	rely	trophy
chicle	language	praise	resin	tune

Across

1. chew
6. something for the head
8. depend on
9. well-liked
12. wiggle
14. a song
15. to bubble
16. trustworthy
18. spoken words

Down

2. antique
3. what makes gum chewy
4. a prize; a silver cup
5. did not get what was expected
7. to grow from a seed
8. comfort; a better feeling
10. sap of a spruce tree
11. very surprised
13. to stop doing something
17. compliments

Animal Disguises

The colors of animals have important uses. They help an animal protect itself from enemies by letting it blend into its background. The colors of animals can also help them survive by warning their enemies that this particular animal has a horrible taste or a powerful, harmful sting. Colors also help animals increase the number of their species by letting the babies blend into their surroundings and remain hidden.

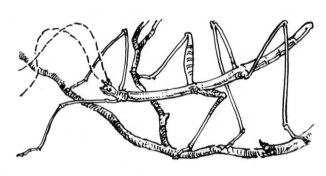
The walking-stick, or stick insect, has a body shape that can be mistaken for a twig. Some stick insects even have green wings that look like leaves. The walking-stick is two to three inches long and a green or brown color.

There is an unusual fish found in the Amazon that looks like a dead leaf. Its transparent, small fins help it move unnoticed to get close to its food—smaller fish. If the Amazon fish gets caught in a net, it lies flat and remains still, looking like a dead leaf. Usually it is tossed back into the water.

There is a small toad found in South America that also resembles a leaf. This flat toad has a sharp snout like the pointed end of a leaf. On its green back, it even has a vein down the middle like the midrib of a leaf. Two small black spots on this toad could easily be mistaken for holes in a leaf that has fallen from a tree.

_____ Title

I. Uses of animal body colors _____

    A. _____

    B. _____

    C. _____

II. Walking-stick _____

    A. _____

    B. _____

    C. _____

    D. _____

III. _____

    A. Transparent, small fins unnoticed as it nears prey

    B. _____

    C. _____

IV. _____

    A. _____

    B. Vein like a midrib of a leaf

    C. _____

D Professor Cambria and Professor Reed made a study of venomous sea animals. They put their findings on a graph. Study the graph and then answer the questions.

Where Venom Is Stored in Sea Animals

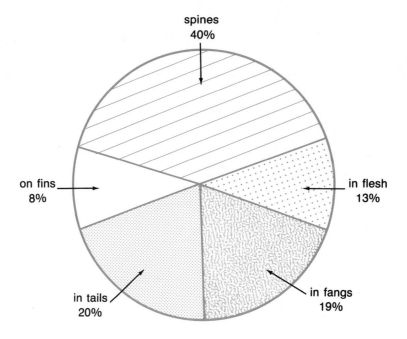

1. In which place do most of the sea animals store venom? _____

2. In which two places do almost the same number of sea animals store venom?

   _____

3. Which is the least used place to store venom? _____

4. What percentage does the whole circle represent? _____

5. What percentage of the sea creatures store venom in their flesh?

   _____

6. What do you know about 40 percent of these sea animals?

   _____

7. How much greater is the number of sea animals that have spines covered with venom than those that store venom in their tails?

   _____

8. What information does this graph show?

   _____

Without water, nothing could live. All living creatures must have it for many different purposes. Some use it for food, others as their home, and others for recreation.

Water is all around you. You have known it since you were an infant. Now here is a challenge. How much do you actually know about water? Think carefully and answer the following questions.

A Here are some words that you need to recognize and understand when reading about water. Choose a word from the waterfall to complete each sentence. If necessary, check reference sources.

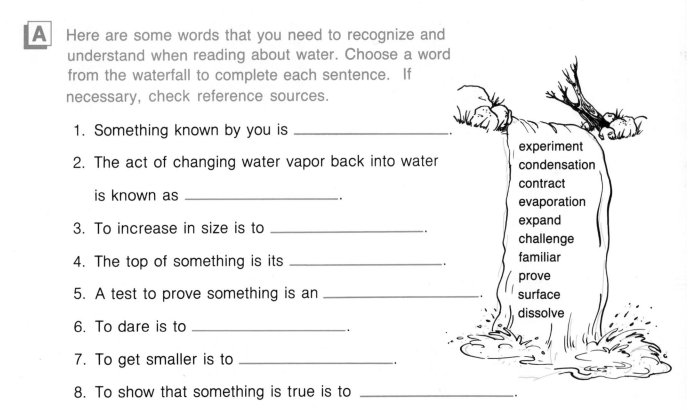

experiment
condensation
contract
evaporation
expand
challenge
familiar
prove
surface
dissolve

1. Something known by you is _____.

2. The act of changing water vapor back into water

    is known as _____.

3. To increase in size is to _____.

4. The top of something is its _____.

5. A test to prove something is an _____.

6. To dare is to _____.

7. To get smaller is to _____.

8. To show that something is true is to _____.

9. The act of changing water into water vapor is known as

    _____.

B The parents have been invited to a program given by the science class. Six of the students are going to show some experiments about water. Here are the students and what they are planning to prove. Pick the correct experiment for each young scientist. Write the letter of the experiment next to the student who did it.

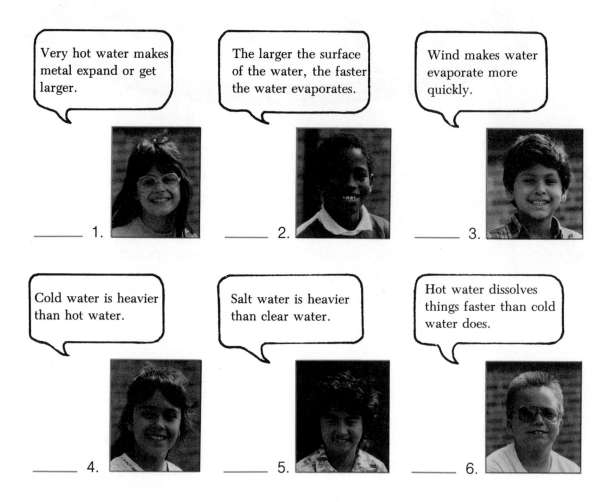

Very hot water makes metal expand or get larger.

_____ 1.

The larger the surface of the water, the faster the water evaporates.

_____ 2.

Wind makes water evaporate more quickly.

_____ 3.

Cold water is heavier than hot water.

_____ 4.

Salt water is heavier than clear water.

_____ 5.

Hot water dissolves things faster than cold water does.

_____ 6.

a. Use two slates or small blackboards. Make both of them wet at the same time. Let one dry naturally. Have an electric fan blowing on the other.

b. Have two glasses of exactly the same size and shape. Use a measuring cup to pour one cup of cold water in the first glass. Using protective mitts on your hands, pour hot water into the measuring cup. Empty the cup of hot water into the other glass. Drop a cube of sugar into each glass at the same time.

c. Buy a small, unopened jar of food. Be certain the lid on the jar is hard to open. Turn the jar upside-down in a wide glass bowl. Protecting your hands with mitts, pour enough hot water into the bowl to touch the lid only. Do not let the hot water fall on the jar. Do not put enough hot water in to reach the glass of the jar. You just want the lid in hot water. Wait two minutes, then remove the jar. Try to open the lid now.

d. Put cold water into a little jar with a small opening. Add red food coloring to the cold water. With mitts to protect your hands, fill a large, deep glass bowl with hot water. Cover the opening of the bottle with your thumb. Lay the jar on its side on top of the hot water. Take away your thumb and let the cold, colored water pour out.

e. Fill a small glass bowl with hot water. Drop a fresh egg into the bowl. It sinks to the bottom. Now stir at least a glassful of salt into the water. Wait a while for the salt to dissolve. The egg rises to the top of the bowl.

f. Get a small cake pan, a small glass bowl, and a narrow vase. Using a measuring cup, pour one cup of water in each container. Leave them on the same table for three days. Then pour the water from each, one at a time, into the measuring cup. How much water is left in the cake pan? How much is left in the bowl? How much is left in the narrow vase? Is the amount the same in each?

C   Read carefully and recall what you have learned about water. See what conclusions you can draw about the following experiments. Predict some outcomes. Underline the correct answer for each question.

Experiment I

3 hours later

1. What happens when water becomes very, very cold?
   a. It dissolves.   b. It condenses.
   c. It freezes.   d. It evaporates.

2. Very, very cold water changes its form. It becomes a
   a. gas.   b. solid.
   c. tension.   d. liquid.

3. The liquid form of water is called
   a. water.   b. water vapor.
   c. ice.   d. steam.

4. As a gas, water is called
   a. water vapor.   b. tension.
   c. solid.   d. ice.

91

5. The solid form of water is known as
   a. freeze.   b. condensation.
   c. water vapor.   d. ice.

6. When water changes into water vapor, it is
   a. freezing.   b. dissolving.
   c. tensing.   d. evaporating.

7. Water in its solid form
   a. contracts.   b. expands.
   c. tenses.   d. decreases in size.

8. There is a bowl of water on the table. As the water changes its form into water vapor, the amount of water in the bowl
   a. increases.   b. does not change.
   c. condenses.   d. decreases.

9. There is a bowl of water on the table. As the water changes its form into a solid, the size of the water
   a. does not change.   b. becomes less.
   c. increases.   d. decreases.

10. In Experiment I, why would the lid of the cup have been pushed off?
    a. The cup had been carelessly placed in the freezer.
    b. The ice contracted.
    c. The ice expanded.
    d. The water vapor pushed it up.

Experiment II

1. What is happening to the water in the pan?
   a. Nothing is happening.
   b. The water is getting cooler.
   c. The temperature is falling.
   d. The temperature is rising.

2. The water in the pan is changing its form. It is becoming a
   a. gas.   b. solid.
   c. tension.   d. liquid.

3. The water still in the pan is a
   a. solid.   b. liquid.
   c. gas.   d. condense.

4. Putting the ladle into the freezer made
   a. the ladle evaporate.
   b. the ladle dissolve.
   c. the temperature of the ladle go down.
   d. the temperature of the ladle rise.

5. When the water vapor touched the ladle, it changed its form and
   became a
   a. tension.
   b. solid.
   c. liquid.
   d. gas.

6. In the picture, the water vapor hits the ladle and starts to
   a. dissolve.   b. tense.
   c. condense.   d. evaporate.

7. What does this experiment show us?
   a. how to increase the size of water
   b. how rain happens
   c. how to prevent rain
   d. how to decrease the size of water

8. Which of these is true about hot water?
   a. It is heavier than cold water.
   b. It weighs the same as cold water.
   c. It is lighter than cold water.
   d. It has more salt in it than cold water.

Label what is described in each story. Use the labels **evaporation** or **condensation**.

_____ 1. On a table in a warm room was a glass full of ice cubes. Margaret put a piece of plastic and a rubber band around the top of the glass. Thirty minutes later, the outside of the glass had drops of water all over it. The drops of water rolled down the glass and made a wet ring around it.

_____ 2. Margaret removed the plastic covering from the glass. She left the ice cubes and the water in the glass. She meant to clean up, but her mother called her. The family went away for two days. When Margaret returned, the glass was not full any more.

_____ 3. Richard took the wet clothes from one machine. He put them into another machine and set the dial. Twenty minutes later, he took the clothes out. They felt dry.

_____ 4. When the rain stopped, Marvin ran out on the sand. There was a big puddle of water near a rock. Marvin saw tiny animals swimming in the water. The sun got hotter and hotter. Marvin went in for lunch. Two hours later, he returned. The puddle had shrunk. Most of the small creatures had disappeared. By three o'clock the puddle also was gone.

_____ 5. Outside a blizzard was howling. Inside it was warm and cozy. The hot air of the room touched the cold windows. By morning, there was ice all over the inside of the windows.

11

We're back! The detective team of Donna and Nicky is here to solve another mystery. Our latest case involved our father's friend, Lester Judd. We went to visit him recently and he told us this puzzling tale.

A few months ago in England, an unexpected discovery had been made. In cleaning out the attic of an ancient house, someone had found a secret closet in the wall. About a hundred early photographs were found in it. They had been taken and dated in 1860 and 1861 by a man named Archer. Dad said that Mr. Archer had been an important person in the early history of photography. People had written about him in books, encyclopedias, and newspapers.

Experts had examined the paper, the chemicals, and the kinds of negatives used. As far as they could tell, everything was what the early photographers had used in the 1860s. Because Archer's photographs were so rare, many collectors wanted them. Mr. Judd had the chance to buy a few of them for $60,000.

I almost fell out of my chair. Dad's hobby was taking pictures. Could it be that a hundred years from now, Dad's photos could be worth that much?

"This is very exciting, Lester. I can hardly wait to set eyes upon these antiques," Dad said to Mr. Judd.

"They're all studies of young street waifs," said Mrs. Judd.

"What are **waifs**?" interrupted Nicky.

Mr. Judd explained. Back in the late 1800s in London, many poor children lived alone in the streets. They were called waifs. They had no parents and no one to care for them. They slept in alleys and empty buildings. For food, they either stole, begged, or starved. Sometimes they earned a few pennies doing hard work.

Nicky and I could not really believe that children could be treated so wickedly. When Mrs. Judd took out a folder of faded photos, we joined Dad in looking at them.

"Ohh!" we exclaimed as we studied the pictures of ragged, mistreated waifs.

Two pictures of the same little girl interested me. She was beautiful with huge, light eyes. In one picture, I saw her back as she struggled with a heavy wheelbarrow. Her hair was a mop of dirty tangles hanging almost to her waist. Nicky was more interested in a photo of a skinny boy holding a torn coat around him. Both children looked starved and sad.

"The experts are right," said Dad. "The materials seem to be the correct ones for 1860. I've seen some of Archer's photos in a museum. They had the same sort of brownish coloring."

Mr. Judd said, "But none of the experts will state positively that these are real Archer photographs and not forgeries. I would like to buy them, but I'm afraid."

Then the Judds started to talk about another expert from Washington, D.C., who was going to arrive on Monday to test the old pictures.

"If they're not forgeries, I wish I had enough money to buy one," Dad said. "I would love to have it in my collection."

Nicky could not stop examining the photos of waifs. We

were not allowed to handle the pictures, but Mrs. Judd spread them out so that we could see them better. I only looked again to see what Nicky was staring at for so long.

Finally Nicky spoke. "I don't know what it is, but there's something wrong with the wrinkles in the kids' clothes."

"Oh, come on, Nick. What can you know about 1860?" I replied.

Then I suddenly realized that I wasn't doing what I always told everyone else to do. To be a detective, you must look and listen carefully and then think. I started to listen carefully to my brother.

"What do you mean?" I asked, bending over the pictures once more.

Nicky pointed to the beautiful, little girl. "Look at those messy, ragged clothes. But in with all the wrinkles, under her hair, I can just make out two straight lines."

I could hardly tell what he was looking at. "Do you have a magnifying glass?" I asked Mrs. Judd.

She laughed, but she handed us one.

"It's on the boy, too," Nicky whispered to me. "It is strange."

We peered through the magnifying glass. I got excited. Nicky was right. I saw something else that seemed out of place. I said nothing aloud, because I didn't want the Judds to laugh at us. Dad might be embarrassed.

Nicky and I needed to check some of the odd things we had noticed on the pictures. We looked in the last volume of the Judds' encyclopedia. Some of what we were looking for was not in the encyclopedia. We were lucky, though. We found enough information by using the index in another book.

Nicky and I decided we would tell Dad what we had discovered. Then he could tell the Judds. We were afraid they would think we were silly. But our plan, as usual, did not work exactly right.

Mrs. Judd came in and inquired, "Are you ready to report your expert findings yet?" She looked at us. The expression on her face seemed to say, "Let's be patient with these kids playing detective."

I said, "Yes, but we may be wrong, because it's hard to see much on those dirty, creased clothes. There is something unusual here. Nicky noticed that usually the wrinkles go in all directions, but there are also little lines that go only straight up and down. On the back of the pretty, little girl, almost hidden by her long, filthy hair, we saw the same straight lines. With the magnifying glass, we figured out that she has a long zipper down the back of her dress. See it there." I pointed.

"Most of the shots of her show the front only, so it is hard to notice. Once we knew what to look for, we found that all the boy waifs have zippers on their clothes, too. Only tiny parts of them can be seen." I stopped.

Then Nicky started, "Zippers weren't invented until 1893. They were first used on clothes in 1931. Kids in 1860 could not have had zippers. The photos have to be forgeries. Donna noticed something, too. See the skinny, little waif who looks as if he is starving?"

I reported on my find. "The clawlike hands holding the ragged coat around the waif's bony chest hardly show. With the magnifying glass, though, you can just see the end of one of those sticky bandages you put on cuts and scrapes. In one of Mr. Judd's books, we read that they weren't invented until the 1940s."

"Someone dishonest is playing a trick on old photo collectors!" exclaimed Dad.

What compliments were showered on us! Mr. and Mrs. Judd piled praise on Nicky and me until even our proud father turned red with embarrassment.

Mr. Judd joked, "I could have lost a lot of money. Instead of paying an expert to fly in from Washington, I should have asked Donna and Nicky for help. I am very grateful to you."

Underline the correct answer for each question.

1. What did Mr. Judd want to buy?

   a. some beautiful photographs from George Washington's time

   b. some of the first photographs ever taken

   c. some pictures showing how children are being mistreated in England

   d. some new cameras that could take pictures faster, clearer, and better than the ones we now have

2. Experts had studied the pictures. What are **experts**?

   a. people who have been successful photographers

   b. people who know a little about many subjects

   c. people whose main work is finding forgeries

   d. people who know a lot about a subject

3. According to Mr. Judd's story, in 1861

   a. photography was in its most popular period.

   b. the art of photography was in its early stages.

   c. photography was invented.

   d. photographers used the same materials and equipment as they do today.

4. Why was Mr. Judd worried about buying the photographs?

   a. He did not have enough money to get the expensive photos.

   b. The photos were the wrong color and too faded to be Archer's photographs.

   c. The paper the pictures were printed on was not the kind used in 1860.

   d. He was not certain the pictures had really been taken by Archer in 1860.

5. What did Donna and Nicky discover about the photographs?

   a. They were forgeries.

   b. They were too wrinkled.

   c. They were too faded.

   d. They had Archer's signature hidden in creases on the clothing.

6. What had Nicky noticed that seemed strange to him?

   a. not enough wrinkles

   b. too many creases

   c. perfectly straight wrinkles

   d. The children on the photos wore nice clothes.

7. What important clues helped Donna and Nicky solve this case?

    a. seeing the wrong kind of zippers on the clothing

    b. seeing that the zippers were in the wrong places

    c. seeing the clothing fastened by sticky bandages for cuts

    d. seeing things on the pictures that had not yet been invented in 1860

8. The two young detectives were not sure what the clues meant. How did they check their information?

    a. by asking experts   b. by calling the library

    c. by researching   d. by guessing

9. What is the main idea of this story?

    a. Reading an encyclopedia can change a child into a photography expert.

    b. Examine everything carefully before buying.

    c. Photography is a popular hobby.

    d. An old photograph is valuable.

10. The photographs were supposed to be of

    a. lovely English gardens.

    b. poor, homeless children.

    c. ancient homes and clothes.

    d. secret closets in attics.

B On each line are two words that are antonyms or opposite in meaning. Circle the antonyms.

1.	towards	across	beneath	away from
2.	pouring	difficult	simple	flooded
3.	creased	repaired	broke	exchanged
4.	strange	odd	arrive	familiar
5.	earth	early	late	invisible
6.	behind	farther	upon	closer
7.	supply	tumble	mumble	shout
8.	piled on	unloaded	unwashed	hugged
9.	huge	filthy	starved	spotless
10.	ordered	inquired	invented	replied
11.	completed	struggled	started	commanded

100

C Choose a word from below to complete each sentence.

forgeries   positively   rare
photography   peer   miserable
compliment   filthy   report
mistreat   struggled   realized
magnify   creases   antique

1. To make something larger to see it more clearly is to _____.

2. Someone who is very unhappy, upset, or ill is _____.

3. False copies that claim to be the real thing are _____.

4. Another word for surely or certainly is _____.

5. Something that is very unclean is _____.

6. To tell about an event is to _____ it.

7. The act of taking pictures with a camera is called

   _____

8. To treat badly is to _____.

9. A _____ is a form of praise.

10. An object used long ago is known as an _____.

11. Wrinkles are also called _____.

12. Something that is seldom seen or not common is _____.

13. To examine something closely, you _____ at it.

14. The photograph will be easier to see if we _____ it.

15. The teacher asked us to make an oral _____.

D A **time line** is a good way to put events in the correct order. It can also be used to organize some kinds of materials into a shorter, more easily readable form. To fill out a time line, you must understand dates. Start with the earliest date at the left of the line and continue adding dates in order until the latest date is at the right end of the line. Place these dates in the correct places on the time line. Then complete the time chart below and on page 103 by placing the events and their dates in correct order.

The History of Cameras

1720—The idea of using film to take pictures started.

1568—A lens was placed on the hole in a box for a clearer view. The picture was reversed.

1830—Daguerre learned how to take a picture that lasted. It took an hour to make the photograph.

1850—Archer invented a better way to make negatives.

1822—Photographs were printed on a glass plate. It took eight hours to make the picture.

1569—A mirror was placed behind the lens in the box so pictures would not be reversed.

1841—Talbot invented the negative so that pictures could be copied over and over.

Time Line

Time Chart

Date	Event
1553	A box with a hole in it was made to focus a picture for artists.

 When looking up information, you usually find many facts about a subject. Some are relevant for what you need. Some are not relevant. **Relevant** means **important for your purposes**.

Read the problem below. Put an **X** by each fact that is not relevant.

Elizabeth Drake was the daughter of wealthy parents. In 1878, she read about the homeless waifs in a large English city. Elizabeth decided to start a soup kitchen, a place where children could be fed a free meal each day.

1. Elizabeth's grandmother gave her a large sum of money to buy meat, fish, and potatoes.
2. Many waifs could be found in the alleys around the harbor.
3. A merchant offered some land he owned near the harbor to use as a small park for the children of Elizabeth's friends and their nursemaids.
4. Elizabeth's parents gave her a trip to France for her eighteenth birthday.
5. Elizabeth's uncle let her live with him free of charge.
6. There was an empty store on a street facing the harbor that could be used as a soup kitchen.
7. Some of Elizabeth's cousins offered to spend one day a week helping at the soup kitchen.
8. Grocers gave free stale bread and leftover vegetables to use in the soup.

SKILLS REVIEW (Stories 10-11)

A Read the following article. Then prepare an outline. Use the main topic of each paragraph. Add subtopics and additional information. The topic box will help you. The beginning of the outline is done for you.

_____ **Topic Box** _____

Scrub skin with strong laundry detergent.	Cover arms, hands, and neck.
Stem	Oil on pets' fur
Damp, red, swollen skin	Terrible itching
Leaves	Flowers
Signs of poison ivy rash	Wash skin several times.
Bark	Ways of preventing poison ivy
Wear heavy shoes and socks.	Rash for one to three weeks
Berries	Oil in every part of plant
Launder clothes separately right away.	Recognize and avoid plant.
	Roots
Oil in smoke of burning ivy	White blisters on skin

The Itching Rash

Poison ivy rash is caused by an oil called *urushiol*. This oil is found in every part of the poison ivy plant—the leaves, the flowers, the berries, the back, the stem, and even the roots. Burning the plant can cause people to become ill, because the smoke is full of urushiol. A pet that has brushed against the leaves of poison ivy gets the oil on its fur. When the owner touches the pet, the result can be a poison ivy rash.

These are the signs of poison ivy rash. A day or two after getting the oil on their skin, human beings develop white blisters that itch terribly. When the blisters open, the skin becomes damp. The blistered parts of the body swell and turn red. Scratching the moist, pink swelling can spread the rash to the fingers and hands. The rash lasts from one to three weeks.

There are several ways to prevent poison ivy rash. First, learn to recognize the plant so you can avoid it. The plant has pointed leaves in groups of three. When hiking or working in bushy, leafy areas, wear heavy socks and sturdy shoes.

Keep the arms, hands, and neck covered. If you have had to walk in a poison ivy area, scrub your skin right away with laundry soap or detergent. Wash several times, because it is difficult to remove the dangerous oil. Clothing should be laundered separately right away also.

_____ (Title)

I. Rash caused by an oil called urushiol _____

   A. _____

       1. _____

       2. _____

       3. _____

       4. _____

       5. _____

       6. _____

   B. _____

   C. _____

II. _____

   A. _____

   B. _____

   C. _____

   D. _____

III. _____

   A. _____

   B. _____

   C. _____

   D. _____

   E. _____

Study the bar graph below and then answer the questions.

How People Got Poison Ivy Rash in Kansas and Nebraska

Places	People	0	500	1000	1500	2000
	Camping in woods	███	███	███	███	
	Playing in parks	███	███			
	Mowing grass	███	███	███		
	Petting dogs	███	██			
	Burning leaves	███	███	███	██	
	Going barefoot	███	███	█		

1. How many people got poison ivy rash by petting a dog? _____

2. In all, how many cases of poison ivy were studied in this graph? _____

3. How many people got the rash by camping in the woods? _____

4. How many more people got the rash by mowing grass than by playing in the parks? _____

5. How many fewer people got poison ivy by going barefoot than by burning leaves? _____

6. How many more people got the rash by camping in the woods than by petting dogs? _____

7. Next to camping in the woods, which way did most people get poison ivy?

   _____

8. What is this graph showing? _____

   _____

Read the circle graph and answer the questions below it.

Places Visited by School Children in Washington, D.C.

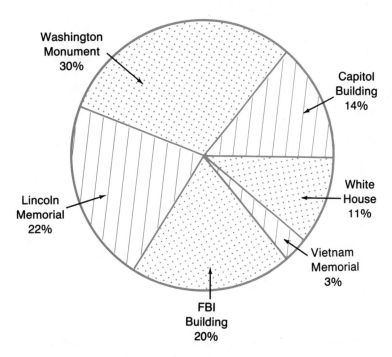

Washington Monument 30%

Capitol Building 14%

White House 11%

Lincoln Memorial 22%

Vietnam Memorial 3%

FBI Building 20%

1. What percentage would half of the graph be? _____

2. Which place was the most popular with school children?

   _____

3. Which place had the fewest school visitors?

   _____

4. What percentage fewer visitors saw the White House than the Lincoln

   Memorial? _____

5. What does this graph show? _____

   _____

6. What percentage more visitors went to the Washington Monument than to

   the Capitol? _____

7. How does the percentage of visitors to the Capitol compare to the
   percentage of visitors to the White House?

   _____

8. Which two places of interest together had half of the visitors?

   _____

D Circle two antonyms in each group of words below.

1. experiment   contract   dissolve   expand
2. tension   inquired   replied   forgery
3. miserable   uncooperative strange   familiar
4. liquid   condensation   embarrassed   unashamed
5. decrease   crease   cease   increase
6. unafraid   frightened   rare   solid
7. negative   positive   evaporate   complain
8. miserable   happy   hobby   photograph
9. sturdy   moist   continue   dry
10. rare   expert   trusted   undependable
11. decrease   rough   important   gentle

E Place the dates below on the time line in correct order. Then read the dates and information in order so that you will have a better idea about America's history.

1836—Fall of the Alamo
1492—Columbus discovered America.
1918—World War I ended.
1607—Jamestown was founded.
1969—People landed on the moon.
1776—Declaration of Independence
1941—Pearl Harbor was attacked.